The Pillsbury

Chocolate Lover's

Cookbook

Nut Goodie Bars, page 24

The Pillsbury

Chocolate Lover's

Cookbook

Doubleday
New York • London • Toronto • Sydney • Auckland

The Pillsbury Company
Pillsbury Publications

Publisher: Sally Peters
Managing Editor: Diane B. Anderson
Associate Editor: Elaine Christiansen
Project Coordinator: Susanne Mattson
Senior Food Editor: Jackie Sheehan
Recipe Copy Editor: Grace Wells
Contributing Editor: S. J. Thoms & Associates, Inc.
Nutrition Coordinators: Patricia Godfrey, R.D.
                       Diane Christensen
Art Direction and Design: Lynne Dolan, Tad Ware & Company, Inc.
Food Stylist: Barb Standal
Photography: Studio 3
Book Editor: Karen Van Westering

Front Cover Photograph: Creamy Chocolate Lace Cheesecake, page 98

Poppin' Fresh® figure, BAKE-OFF®, Classic® Cookbooks, Pillsbury's BEST®,
Pillsbury Plus®, Hungry Jack®, Pillsbury Frosting Supreme™ and Tunnel of
Fudge™ are registered trademarks of The Pillsbury Company.
Illustration page 7 reprinted with permission from Bettmann Archive.

PUBLISHED BY DOUBLEDAY
a division of Bantam Doubleday Dell Publishing Group, Inc.
666 Fifth Avenue, New York, New York 10103

DOUBLEDAY and the portrayal of an anchor
with a dolphin are trademarks of Doubleday,
a division of Bantam Doubleday Dell Publishing Group, Inc.

Library of Congress Cataloging-in-Publication Data

  The Pillsbury chocolate lover's cookbook.
    p. cm.
  1. Cookery (Chocolate)   I. Pillsbury Company.
  TX767.C5P55   1990
  641.6'374 — dc20   89-29382
                                                      CIP

ISBN 0-385-23869-X

Contents

Make Mine Chocolate

hocolate begins with the *bean* (fruit) of the cacao tree, which grows in lush tropical orchards along the Equator, mainly in Central America and West Africa. The beans are roasted and shelled, leaving the cacao *nibs*, or "meat" of the bean. As the nibs are ground, they form a thick paste of cocoa butter and ground cacao. This is known as *chocolate liquor*. The next processing step depends on the final form desired—cocoa powder or chocolate. Production techniques have been perfected so that a diversity of chocolate products can be created to meet every chocolate connoisseur's needs and desires.

[Leaf, flower, and fruit of the Cacao, with a pod opened.]

Unsweetened Varieties

UNSWEETENED BAKING CHOCOLATE: Pure chocolate with no sugar or flavorings added. The basic chocolate from which all other products are made. Available in 1-ounce squares; sold in packages of 4 or 8 ounces. Primary uses: baking, frostings and confections. Other names: chocolate baking bars or squares.

PREMELTED UNSWEETENED CHOCOLATE: A semi-liquid blend of cocoa and vegetable oil. Available in 8-ounce packages of 1-ounce envelopes. Primary use: substitute for Unsweetened Baking Chocolate.

UNSWEETENED COCOA: A pure chocolate powder with most of the cocoa butter removed. Available in cans of 8 to 16 ounces. Primary uses: beverages, sauces, frostings and baking.

DUTCH-PROCESS COCOA: Made from chocolate liquor that has been treated with an alkali agent to create a darker powder and different flavor from Unsweetened Cocoa. Available in 8.8-ounce boxes. Primary uses: same as Unsweetened Cocoa.

Sweetened Varieties

SWEET COOKING CHOCOLATE: A special blend of (at least 15 percent) chocolate, sugar and cocoa butter. Available in bars of 4 or 8 ounces. Also available in other shapes and sizes; sold in packages of 6 and 12 ounces. Primary uses: baking, confections, garnishes and pastry fillings. Other names: German sweet cooking chocolate or sweet dark chocolate. Other names for pieces: chips, dots, morsels or bits.

SEMI-SWEET CHOCOLATE: A special blend of (at least 35 percent) chocolate, sugar and cocoa butter. Available in squares of 1 or 2 ounces; packed in 8-ounce bars or packages. Also available in pieces ranging in size from mini to large and in "gourmet" chunks; sold in packages of 6 to 24 ounces. Primary uses: same as for Sweet Chocolate. Other names for pieces: chips, dots, morsels, bits or chunks.

BITTERSWEET AND EXTRA-BITTERSWEET CHOCOLATE: A special blend of (at least 55 percent) chocolate, sugar and cocoa butter. Available in specialty shops. Primary uses: same as for Sweet Chocolate.

MILK CHOCOLATE: A blend of (at least 10 percent) chocolate, cocoa butter, sugar and (at least 12 percent) milk solids. Most common forms are candy snacks, such as chocolate bars, foil-wrapped chocolates and novelty shapes. Also formed into regular- and large-size pieces; sold in packages of 10 to 11.5 ounces. Primary uses: same as for Sweet Chocolate. Other names for pieces: chips or morsels.

COATING CHOCOLATE: Chocolate with cocoa butter added. Varieties include sweet, semi-sweet and milk chocolate. Molded into blocks of 1 to 10 pounds; available in specialty shops. Primary use: to create a very high-gloss covering for candy. Other name: couverture.

Additional Varieties

CHOCOLATE LIQUEURS: A blend of chocolate, alcohol and flavorings. Best known is crème de cacao with the familiar chocolate color; white crème de cacao is clear. Mint, almond-cherry and orange-flavored chocolate liqueurs are also available. Bottled in 375- and 750-ml. containers; available where liquor is sold. Primary uses: beverages, desserts and confections.

HOT COCOA MIX: Contains cocoa, milk solids and sugar or artificial sweetener; hot water is added. May include marshmallows. Available in cans and in boxes of 8 to 12 single-serving envelopes. Primary use: hot beverage. (Cannot be substituted for unsweetened cocoa in recipes.)

PRESWEETENED COCOA POWDER: Contains cocoa, sugar or artificial sweetener, and other flavorings; dry milk powder is sometimes added. Available in cans. Primary uses: hot and cold beverages. (Cannot be substituted for unsweetened cocoa in recipes.) Other name: chocolate milk mix.

Chocolate's Cousins

WHITE BAKING BAR: A blend of sugar, milk and flavorings; cocoa butter is included in the better-quality varieties; may contain vegetable oil. Not really chocolate because it does not contain chocolate liquor. Available in white, dark or pastel colors.

Molded into bars and blocks weighing from 1 ounce to 5 pounds. Also formed into regular and large-sized chips; sold in packages of 10 to 12 ounces. Primary uses: baking, candies and frostings. Other names: white chocolate, vanilla milk chips or compound chocolate.

VANILLA-FLAVORED CANDY COATING: A combination of sugar, milk and flavorings plus vegetable fats. It does not contain cocoa butter or chocolate liquor. Molded into 2-ounce blocks; sold in containers of 16 or 24 ounces. Primary uses: candies, glazes and fillings. Other names: almond bark, confectioners' candy coating or confectioners' coating.

CAROB: Made from the ground pod of a tree found in the Mediterranean region. Available as chips, powder, coating for candy and snack bars. Primary use: alternative flavor for those allergic to chocolate. Can sometimes be substituted for chocolate, but generally recipes are specially developed to use carob products. Our recipes have not been tested with carob as a chocolate substitute. Other name: St. John's bread.

CHOCOLATE-FLAVORED: Products that derive their flavor from cocoa and/or chocolate liquor but do not contain enough to be defined as "true" chocolate. They include Chocolate-Flavored Syrup, Chocolate-Flavored Sprinkles, Chocolate-Flavored Candy Coating and Chocolate-Flavored Pieces.

IMITATION OR ARTIFICIAL CHOCOLATE: Contains no chocolate liquor or cocoa butter; may not contain sugar or milk either.

Tips for Cooking with Chocolate

Cook's Notes throughout this cookbook and the following material offer invaluable information about cooking with chocolate.

Storing Chocolate and Cocoa

Store chocolate in a cool, dry place — about 60 to 75°F. and less than 50 percent humidity. Chocolate can be refrigerated if tightly wrapped. This will keep it from absorbing odors from other foods and prevent moisture from condensing on its surface when the chocolate is removed from the refrigerator. Chocolate that has been refrigerated will be hard and brittle, so let it stand tightly wrapped at room temperature before use.

Chocolate melts when it is stored at temperatures higher than 75°F., causing the cocoa butter to rise to the surface. The gray film that results is called "cocoa butter bloom." And when condensation occurs on semi-sweet or milk chocolate, the sugar can dissolve and rise to the surface as "sugar bloom." Neither bloom affects the quality or flavor of the chocolate. The original color will return when the chocolate is used in cooking or baking.

Although less sensitive to storage conditions, cocoa should be kept in a tightly covered container in a cool, dry place. Cocoa tends to become lumpy and lighter in color when stored at high temperatures or high humidity.

Melting Chocolate

UTENSILS: Make sure they are clean and dry. Small amounts of moisture on utensils can cause chocolate to become stiff or grainy during melting. This is called "seizing." To return the chocolate to a smooth consistency, add 1 teaspoon solid vegetable shortening (not butter or margarine) for every 2 ounces of chocolate. Using a wire whisk will help to achieve a smooth consistency.

PIECE SIZE: To speed melting, break or chop chocolate blocks, bars or chunks into smaller, uniform pieces.

MELTING ON THE RANGE TOP: Use a heavy saucepan and low, even heat (below 110°F.). Stir constantly to avoid scorching and stiffening.

MELTING IN THE MICROWAVE OVEN: Melt chocolate in an uncovered microwave-safe container. A 1-ounce square will require 1 to 2 minutes on MEDIUM; add 10 seconds for each additional ounce. One cup (6 ounces) of pieces (chips) needs 2½ to 3½ minutes on MEDIUM; add 2 to 3 minutes for each additional cup. Most chocolates will become glossy and not appear to be melted because they retain their original shape until stirred. Stir until completely melted and smooth. Add more time only if chocolate is not completely melted.

TEMPERING CHOCOLATE: Tempering is a method of melting and cooling chocolate for superior-quality dipped chocolates. The chocolate becomes easy to handle and stays firm and glossy at room temperature. Tempering will also prevent bloom. The following process needs to be done very slowly.

To temper, chop 1 pound, or desired amount, of semi-sweet, unsweetened or sweet cooking chocolate into small pieces. Place pieces in the top of a double boiler. Fill the bottom of the double boiler with hot water (110 to 120°F). Place double boiler top so that its bottom just barely touches the water. As the chocolate begins to melt, stir it frequently. You may need to change the water to keep it hot

enough. Continue melting until the temperature of the chocolate reaches 110 to 120°F.

Fill the bottom of the double boiler with cool water (60 to 70°F.). Replace the double boiler top and stir the chocolate constantly until it reaches a temperature of 80 to 83°F. Fill the bottom of the double boiler with lukewarm water (78 to 80°F.). Keep the chocolate at this temperature while dipping. Throughout the tempering process make sure that no moisture gets into the chocolate.

Chocolate Substitutions

Recipes in this cookbook have been developed and tested using the type of chocolate specified. It's always best to follow the recipe as written. Of course, there will be times when you want to substitute one flavor of chocolate pieces for another. And in an emergency you may need to use what's on hand in the kitchen. It's not possible to substitute sweetened cocoa mixes in recipes that call for unsweetened cocoa. There are other substitutions that can be made successfully.

When a recipe calls for melted chocolate, here are some guidelines.

Substitutions for Melted Chocolate

If the recipe calls for . . .	You can substitute . . .
1 ounce (1 square) unsweetened chocolate	1 ounce (1 envelope) premelted unsweetened chocolate — or — 3 tablespoons unsweetened cocoa plus 1 tablespoon cooking oil or melted shortening
6 ounces (1 cup) semi-sweet chocolate chips	6 tablespoons unsweetened cocoa plus ¼ cup sugar and ¼ cup cooking oil or melted shortening — or — 6 ounces (6 squares) semi-sweet chocolate
1 ounce (1 square) semi-sweet chocolate	1 ounce (1 square) unsweetened chocolate plus 1 tablespoon sugar — or — 3 tablespoons semi-sweet chocolate chips
4 ounces (4 squares) sweet cooking chocolate	¼ cup unsweetened cocoa plus ⅓ cup sugar and 3 tablespoons cooking oil or melted shortening

Pictured top to bottom: Favorite Fudge Brownies, page 12; Midnight Munchers, page 21

Brownies & Bars

When someone says, "I'll bring bars," you know that dessert is well taken care of and that it will be delicious.

Brownies and bars can be just about anything you want them to be. They can be toted anywhere as a much-appreciated contribution to a potluck meal or packed in a pretty box to say "thank you" to your hostess. For a show-off dessert, you can choose an elegant concoction such as the multilayered Orange Cappuccino Bars or Grasshopper Brownies. Or when you're looking for a snack that can be made in minutes using little more than a bowl, spoon and baking pan, try Crunchy Snack Bars or Chocolate Chunk Pecan Brownies.

The most popular of all bars are brownies in all their rich variations, from moist and cakelike to chewy and fudgy. Some say that brownies were originally a fallen chocolate cake, while other food historians believe they are a takeoff on a chocolate variety of Scottish tea scones. Whatever their origin, brownies have won the hearts of Americans.

In this chapter, you'll find brownie squares, wedges, bars and even hearts. Flavor combinations will intrigue and delight—chocolate teamed with banana and mocha flavors, cashew-studded blond brownies with a rich caramel taste, and the double-chocolate pleasure of brownies filled with chunks of chocolate. For those who want to temper their indulgence, we have included Choco-Lite Brownies made with less fat and sugar.

This collection offers made-from-scratch brownies and bars as well as recipes that take advantage of convenience products and methods, such as microwaving. Some recipes make big pans of treats ideal for a crowd, while others are sized just right for a smaller family. And you won't find a recipe in the whole lot of them that you don't like!

CHOCOLATE SYRUP MICROWAVE BROWNIES

FAVORITE FUDGE BROWNIES

Chocolate Syrup Microwave Brownies

When having last-minute guests, this is an easy, cakelike brownie to pop in your microwave. Top each brownie square with vanilla ice cream for a delicious taste treat.

COOK'S NOTE
Restoring Melted Chocolate That Stiffens

A caution when melting chocolate: excessive heat or water drops can cause it to stiffen. Should this happen, stir melted shortening (not butter or margarine) into the stiffened chocolate (1½ teaspoons shortening for each ½ cup chips or 3 ounces of chocolate).

BROWNIES
- ½ cup margarine or butter, softened
- ½ cup sugar
- 2 eggs
- ½ cup chocolate-flavored syrup
- 2 teaspoons vanilla
- ¾ cup all purpose or unbleached flour
- ¼ salt

FROSTING
- 1 cup powdered sugar
- 2 tablespoons chocolate-flavored syrup
- 1 tablespoon margarine or butter, softened
- 2 to 4 teaspoons milk

MICROWAVE DIRECTIONS:
Grease 10 × 6-inch (1½-quart) microwave-safe dish. In medium bowl, combine ½ cup margarine and ½ cup sugar; beat until light and fluffy. Add eggs, ½ cup chocolate-flavored syrup and vanilla; beat well. Lightly spoon flour into measuring cup; level off. Stir in flour and salt. Pour into greased dish. Microwave on MEDIUM for 8 minutes, rotating dish ½ turn halfway through cooking. Microwave on HIGH for 2 to 3 minutes or until center is set. Cool completely on flat surface.

In small bowl combine all frosting ingredients, adding enough milk for desired spreading consistency; beat until smooth. Spread over cooled brownies. Cut into bars. **12 to 16 servings.**

HIGH ALTITUDE – Above 3500 Feet: Increase flour to 1 cup. Bake in greased 9-inch round microwave-safe dish. Microwave on MEDIUM for 8 minutes, rotating dish every 2 minutes. Microwave on HIGH for 1 to 2 minutes or until center is set.

NUTRIENTS PER 1/16 OF RECIPE

Calories	170	Sodium	130mg
Fat	7g	Potassium	45mg
Cholesterol	35mg		

BROWNIES
- 5 ounces (5 squares) unsweetened chocolate, cut into pieces
- ¾ cup butter or margarine
- 1 tablespoon vanilla
- 2¼ cups sugar
- 4 eggs
- 1⅓ cups all purpose or unbleached flour
- 1½ cups coarsely chopped nuts

FROSTING
- 1½ cups powdered sugar
- 2 tablespoons unsweetened cocoa
- ¼ cup butter or margarine, softened
- 2 tablespoons milk
- ½ teaspoon vanilla
  Whole pecans or walnuts, if desired

Heat oven to 375°F. Grease 13 × 9-inch pan. In small saucepan over low heat, melt chocolate and ¾ cup butter, stirring constantly until smooth. Remove from heat. Stir in 1 tablespoon vanilla; set aside.

In large bowl, combine sugar and eggs; beat about 7 minutes or until sugar is dissolved. Lightly spoon flour into measuring cup; level off. Add flour, chocolate mixture and nuts to egg mixture; stir until just blended. Pour batter into greased pan. Bake at 375°F. for 25 to 35 minutes. *Do not overbake.* Cool completely.

In small bowl, combine all frosting ingredients except pecans; blend until smooth. Frost cooled bars. Refrigerate 1 hour. Cut into bars. Garnish each bar with whole pecan. **36 brownies.**

HIGH ALTITUDE – Above 3500 Feet: No change.

NUTRIENTS PER 1 BROWNIE

Calories	190	Sodium	65mg
Fat	12g	Potassium	80mg
Cholesterol	55mg		

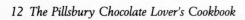

A MOST REQUESTED RECIPE

ZEBRA BROWNIES

FILLING
  2 (3-ounce) packages cream
    cheese, softened
  ¼ cup sugar
  ½ teaspoon vanilla
  1 egg

BROWNIES
21½-ounce package family size
    brownie mix
  ⅓ cup water
  ⅓ cup oil
  1 egg

Heat oven to 350°F. Generously grease bottom only of 13 × 9-inch pan. In small bowl, combine all filling ingredients; beat until smooth. Set aside. In large bowl, combine all brownie ingredients; beat 50 strokes with spoon. Spread half of brownie batter in greased pan. Pour filling mixture over brownie batter, spreading to cover. Top with spoonfuls of remaining brownie batter. To marble, lightly pull knife through batter in wide curves; turn pan and repeat.

Bake at 350°F. for 30 to 35 minutes or until set. *Do not overbake.* Cool completely. Refrigerate at least 1 hour; cut into bars. Store in refrigerator. **36 bars.**

HIGH ALTITUDE — Above 3500 Feet: Add 2 tablespoons flour to dry brownie mix. Bake as directed above.

NUTRIENTS PER 1 BAR

Calories	110	Sodium	80mg
Fat	5g	Potassium	30mg
Cholesterol	20mg		

Zebra Brownies

Delectable and fudgy, this brownie has a marbling of cream cheese.

Clockwise from top left: Grasshopper Brownies; Banana Brownies with Mocha Frosting; Cappuccino Fudge Brownies

BANANA BROWNIES WITH MOCHA FROSTING

BROWNIES
21½-ounce package family-size
  brownie mix
½ cup water
½ cup oil
½ cup (1 large) mashed banana
1 egg
½ cup semi-sweet chocolate chips

FROSTING
3 tablespoons unsweetened cocoa
1 teaspoon instant coffee granules
  or crystals
⅓ cup margarine or butter,
  softened
4 cups powdered sugar
¼ teaspoon salt
1 teaspoon vanilla
5 to 6 tablespoons milk

Heat oven to 350°F. Grease bottom only of 13 × 9-inch pan. In large bowl, combine brownie mix, water, oil, banana and egg; beat 50 strokes with spoon. Stir in chocolate chips. Spread in greased pan. Bake at 350°F. for 28 to 35 minutes. *Do not overbake.* Cool completely.

In large bowl, combine cocoa, instant coffee and margarine; beat until light and fluffy. Add remaining frosting ingredients, adding 1 tablespoon milk at a time for desired spreading consistency. Frost cooled brownies. Cut into bars. **36 brownies.**

HIGH ALTITUDE — Above 3500 Feet: Add ⅓ cup flour to dry brownie mix; decrease oil to ⅓ cup. Bake at 350°F. for 30 to 40 minutes.

NUTRIENTS PER 1 BROWNIE

Calories	170	Sodium	100mg
Fat	7g	Potassium	75mg
Cholesterol	8mg		

CAPPUCCINO FUDGE BROWNIES

BROWNIES
    5 ounces (5 squares) unsweetened
        chocolate, cut into pieces
    ¾ cup butter or margarine
    2 tablespoons instant coffee
        granules or crystals
    1 tablespoon vanilla
    2¼ cups sugar
    1 teaspoon cinnamon
    4 eggs
    1⅓ cups all purpose or unbleached
        flour
    1½ cups coarsely chopped pecans

FROSTING
    ½ cup butter or margarine,
        softened
    2 cups powdered sugar
    2 tablespoons brewed coffee
    ½ teaspoon vanilla

GLAZE
    1 ounce (1 square) semi-sweet
        chocolate
    1 teaspoon shortening

Heat oven to 375°F. Grease 13 × 9-inch pan. In small saucepan over low heat, melt unsweetened chocolate and ¾ cup butter, stirring constantly until smooth. Remove from heat. Stir in instant coffee and 1 tablespoon vanilla; set aside.

In large bowl, combine sugar, cinnamon and eggs; beat about 7 minutes or until sugar is dissolved. Lightly spoon flour into measuring cup; level off. Fold flour, pecans and chocolate mixture into egg mixture until just blended. Spread batter in greased pan. Bake at 375°F. for 25 to 35 minutes. *Do not overbake.* Cool completely.

In small bowl, beat ½ cup butter until light and fluffy. Add remaining frosting ingredients; beat until smooth. Frost cooled brownies.

In small saucepan over low heat, melt semi-sweet chocolate with shortening, stirring constantly until smooth. Drizzle glaze in horizontal parallel lines about 1 inch apart over top of frosted brownies. Immediately draw knife through glaze in straight vertical lines

to form pattern. Refrigerate until firm. Cut into bars. **36 brownies.**

HIGH ALTITUDE—Above 3500 Feet: No change.

NUTRIENTS PER 1 BROWNIE

Calories	220	Sodium	75mg
Fat	13g	Potassium	70mg
Cholesterol	50mg		

GRASSHOPPER BROWNIES

BROWNIES
    21½-ounce package family-size
        brownie mix
    ½ cup water
    ½ cup oil
    1 egg

FILLING
    4 cups powdered sugar
    3-ounce package cream cheese,
        softened
    ¼ cup margarine or butter,
        softened
    3 tablespoons milk
    1 teaspoon vanilla
    ¼ teaspoon peppermint extract
    4 to 6 drops green food coloring

GLAZE
    1 ounce (1 square) unsweetened
        chocolate
    1 tablespoon margarine or butter

Heat oven to 350°F. Grease bottom only of 13 × 9-inch pan. In large bowl, combine all brownie ingredients; beat 50 strokes with spoon. Spread batter in greased pan. Bake at 350°F. for 33 to 35 minutes or until brownies are set. *Do not overbake.* Cool completely.

In large bowl, combine all filling ingredients; beat at medium speed until smooth. Spread over cooled brownies.

In small saucepan over low heat, melt chocolate and 1 tablespoon margarine, stirring constantly until smooth; drizzle over filling. Refrigerate 1 to 2 hours until firm. Cut into bars. Store in refrigerator. **36 brownies.**

HIGH ALTITUDE—Above 3500 Feet: Add ¼ cup flour to dry brownie mix. Bake as directed above.

NUTRIENTS PER 1 BROWNIE

Calories	170	Sodium	85mg
Fat	7g	Potassium	55mg
Cholesterol	10mg		

Cappuccino Fudge Brownies

Cappuccino, a traditional beverage of Italy, is a coffee served with a foamy head of milk or cream. Superb coffee flavor permeates these elegant brownies.

Grasshopper Brownies

This popular brownie with the fluffy mint frosting was originally made with refrigerated spread 'n' bake brownies. This new version is made with brownie mix for quick preparation and rich, fudgy flavor.

ROCKY ROAD FUDGE BARS

BASE

½ cup margarine or butter
1 ounce (1 square) unsweetened chocolate, chopped
1 cup all purpose or unbleached flour
1 cup sugar
1 teaspoon baking powder
1 teaspoon vanilla
2 eggs
¾ cup chopped nuts

FILLING

8-ounce package cream cheese, softened; reserving 2 ounces for frosting
¼ cup margarine or butter, softened
½ cup sugar
2 tablespoons all purpose or unbleached flour
½ teaspoon vanilla
1 egg
¼ cup chopped nuts
6-ounce package (1 cup) semi-sweet chocolate chips

FROSTING

2 cups miniature marshmallows
¼ cup margarine or butter
¼ cup milk
1 ounce (1 square) unsweetened chocolate, chopped
Reserved 2 ounces cream cheese
3 cups powdered sugar, sifted
1 teaspoon vanilla

Heat oven to 350°F. Grease and flour 13 × 9-inch pan. In large saucepan over low heat, melt ½ cup margarine and 1 ounce unsweetened chocolate, stirring constantly until smooth. Lightly spoon flour into measuring cup; level off. Add 1 cup flour and remaining base ingredients; blend well. Spread in greased and floured pan.

In small bowl, combine all filling ingredients except ¼ cup nuts and chocolate chips. Beat 1 minute at medium speed until smooth and fluffy. By hand, stir in nuts. Spread over chocolate mixture; sprinkle evenly with chocolate chips. Bake at 350°F. for 25 to 35 minutes or until toothpick inserted in center comes out clean. Immediately sprinkle marshmallows over top. Bake an additional 2 minutes.

In large saucepan over low heat, combine ¼ cup margarine, milk, 1 ounce unsweetened chocolate and reserved 2 ounces cream cheese; stir until well blended. Remove from heat. Stir in powdered sugar and 1 teaspoon vanilla until smooth. Immediately pour frosting over marshmallows and lightly swirl with knife to marble. Refrigerate until firm. Cut into bars. Store in refrigerator. **48 bars.**

HIGH ALTITUDE — Above 3500 Feet: No change.

NUTRIENTS PER 1 BAR

Calories	160	Sodium	70mg
Fat	9g	Potassium	50mg
Cholesterol	20mg		

Chocolate Chunk Pecan Brownies

This culinary inspiration was developed for chocoholics. It is a moist, nut-textured, intensely flavored brownie that will satisfy any chocolate craving — at least for a little while.

COOK'S NOTE
Cocoa

Recipes requiring cocoa refer to the unsweetened type, not instant cocoa mix or other combinations containing sweeteners. Break up any cocoa lumps and measure it as you do flour and sugar, by spooning lightly into measuring cup and leveling off with a straight-edged spatula or knife.

CHOCOLATE CHUNK PECAN BROWNIES

1 cup margarine or butter
2 cups sugar
2 teaspoons vanilla
4 eggs, slightly beaten
1 cup all purpose or unbleached flour
½ cup unsweetened cocoa
½ teaspoon salt
8 ounces (8 squares) semi-sweet chocolate, coarsely chopped
1 cup chopped pecans

Heat oven to 350°F. Grease 13 × 9-inch pan. Melt margarine in medium saucepan over low heat. Add sugar, vanilla and eggs; blend well. Lightly spoon flour into measuring cup; level off. Stir in flour, cocoa and salt; blend well. Add chocolate and pecans. Pour into greased pan. Bake at 350°F. for 30 to 40 minutes or until set. Cool completely. Cut into bars. **36 brownies.**

HIGH ALTITUDE — Above 3500 Feet: No change.

NUTRIENTS PER 1 BROWNIE

Calories	170	Sodium	105mg
Fat	10g	Potassium	55mg
Cholesterol	30mg		

Choco-Lite Brownies

CHOCO-LITE BROWNIES

⅔ cup all purpose or unbleached
   flour
¾ cup sugar
⅓ cup unsweetened cocoa
¼ teaspoon baking powder
¼ teaspoon salt
⅓ cup margarine, melted
2 teaspoons vanilla
2 eggs, slightly beaten
   Powdered sugar

Heat oven to 350°F. Grease and flour bottom only of 8-inch square pan. Lightly spoon flour into measuring cup; level off. In large bowl, combine flour, sugar, cocoa, baking powder and salt; blend well. Add margarine, vanilla and eggs; stir just to combine. Pour into greased and floured pan. Bake at 350°F. for 18 to 23 minutes or until set. *Do not overbake.* Sprinkle with powdered sugar. **24 brownies.**

HIGH ALTITUDE — Above 3500 Feet: Increase flour to ¾ cup.

NUTRIENTS PER 1 BROWNIE

Calories	70	Sodium	70mg
Fat	3g	Potassium	20mg
Cholesterol	25mg		

Choco-Lite Brownies

Our tasters couldn't believe that these rich, moist, chocolaty brownies were lower in fat and calories than many brownies.

Fudgy Caramel Wedges

FUDGY CARAMEL WEDGES

BASE
   2 ounces (2 squares) semi-sweet chocolate, chopped
   1 ounce (1 square) unsweetened chocolate, chopped
   ½ cup margarine or butter
   ¾ cup all purpose or unbleached flour
   ¾ cup sugar
   1 tablespoon vanilla
   2 eggs
   ½ cup coarsely chopped pecans

TOPPING
   10 caramels, unwrapped
   2 tablespoons milk
   ½ ounce (½ square) unsweetened chocolate, chopped
   2 teaspoons margarine or butter
   1 teaspoon light corn syrup

Heat oven to 325°F. Line 9-inch round cake pan with foil; grease. In medium saucepan over low heat, melt semi-sweet chocolate, 1 ounce unsweetened chocolate and ½ cup margarine, stirring constantly until smooth. Cool slightly. Lightly spoon flour into measuring cup; level off. Stir in flour, sugar, vanilla and eggs; blend well. Spread in greased, foil-lined pan. Sprinkle pecans over batter. Bake at 325°F. for 20 to 30 minutes or until set. Cool 10 minutes; carefully remove base from pan. Remove foil from base.

In small saucepan over low heat, melt caramels and milk, stirring frequently until smooth. Drizzle over base. In same saucepan over low heat, melt ½ ounce unsweetened chocolate, 2 teaspoons margarine and corn syrup, stirring frequently until smooth. Drizzle over caramel. Cool completely. Cut into wedges. **12 to 16 servings.**

MICROWAVE DIRECTIONS:
Grease 8-inch (1½-quart) round microwave-safe dish. Line bottom with waxed paper; grease again. In another 1½-quart microwave-safe bowl, combine semi-sweet chocolate, 1 ounce unsweetened chocolate and ½ cup margarine. Microwave on MEDIUM for 2 to 3 minutes, stirring once halfway through cooking. Stir until smooth. Cool slightly. Lightly spoon flour into measuring cup; level off. Stir in flour, sugar, vanilla and eggs; blend well. Pour into greased, waxed paper-lined dish. Sprinkle pecans over batter. Microwave on MEDIUM for 9 minutes, rotating pan ½ turn twice during cooking. Microwave on HIGH for 2 to 3 minutes or until center is set and top surface just loses wet appearance. Cool 10 minutes; carefully remove base from dish. Remove waxed paper from base.

In 1-cup microwave-safe cup, combine caramels and *1 tablespoon* milk. Microwave on MEDIUM for 1½ to 2 minutes. Stir until smooth. Drizzle over base. In same 1-cup microwave-safe measuring cup, combine ½ ounce unsweetened chocolate, 2 teaspoons margarine and corn syrup. Microwave on MEDIUM for 45 to 60 seconds. Stir until smooth. Drizzle over caramel. Cool completely. Cut into wedges.

HIGH ALTITUDE—Above 3500 Feet: Decrease sugar by 1 tablespoon. Bake at 350°F. for 20 to 30 minutes.

NUTRIENTS PER 1/16 OF RECIPE
Calories	200	Sodium	96mg
Fat	13g	Potassium	80mg
Cholesterol	35mg		

Fudgy Caramel Wedges

This decadent, unusually shaped brownie is perfect for a special occasion but easy enough to prepare any time. Use a very sharp knife to cut pretty wedges.

COOK'S NOTE
Storing Bars

To store bars, place them in a tightly covered container or leave them right in the baking pan and cover it tightly with foil. Store them at room temperature unless the recipe specifies refrigerator storage.

OATMEAL CARMELITAS

GLAZED BROWNIE BARS

Glazed Brownie Bars

Make brownies special by cutting them into heart shapes and dipping them in candy coating. Use your imagination to decorate as you drizzle the glaze over the coated brownies.

CRUST

> 2 cups all purpose or unbleached flour
> 2 cups quick-cooking rolled oats
> 1½ cups firmly packed brown sugar
> 1 teaspoon baking soda
> ½ teaspoon salt
> 1¼ cups margarine or butter, softened

FILLING

> 6-ounce package (1 cup) semi-sweet chocolate chips
> ½ cup chopped nuts
> 12-ounce jar (1 cup) caramel ice cream topping
> 3 tablespoons all purpose or unbleached flour

Heat oven to 350°F. Grease 13 × 9-inch pan. Lightly spoon flour into measuring cup; level off. In large bowl, combine all crust ingredients; blend at low speed until crumbly. Press half of crumb mixture, about 3 cups, in bottom of greased pan. Reserve remaining crumb mixture for topping. Bake at 350°F. for 10 minutes.

Sprinkle warm crust with chocolate chips and nuts. In small bowl, combine caramel topping and 3 tablespoons flour; drizzle evenly over chocolate chips and nuts. Sprinkle with reserved crumb mixture. Bake an additional 18 to 22 minutes or until golden brown. Cool completely. Refrigerate 1 to 2 hours or until filling is set. Cut into bars. **36 bars.**

HIGH ALTITUDE—Above 3500 Feet: No change.

NUTRIENTS PER 1 BAR

Calories	200	Sodium	200mg
Fat	9g	Potassium	80mg
Cholesterol	0mg		

BROWNIE

> 21½-ounce package family-size brownie mix
> ½ cup water
> ½ cup oil
> 1 egg

GLAZE

> 4 ounces chocolate-flavored candy coating, cut into pieces
> 2 teaspoons oil
> 4 ounces vanilla-flavored candy coating, cut into pieces
> 2 teaspoons oil

Heat oven to 350°F. Line 13 × 9-inch pan with foil; grease foil on bottom of pan only. In large bowl, combine all brownie ingredients; beat 50 strokes with spoon. Spread in greased, foil-lined pan. Bake at 350°F. for 33 to 35 minutes or until set. *Do not overbake.* Cool completely. Freeze brownies ½ hour.

Lift brownies from pan using foil; place on cutting board. Using 2½-inch heart-shaped cookie cutter, cut out 8 to 10 brownie hearts. In small saucepan over low heat, melt chocolate-flavored candy coating with 2 teaspoons oil, stirring constantly until smooth. Keep warm. Quickly dip sides of 4 or 5 cut out brownies into melted candy coating. Allow excess to drip off; place on waxed paper. Spoon melted chocolate-flavored candy coating over tops of brownies; smooth with knife.

Repeat process with vanilla-flavored candy coating, 2 teaspoons oil and remaining 4 to 5 brownies. Brownies may need to be dipped and frosted twice to completely cover with vanilla-flavored candy coating. Drizzle small amount of contrasting candy coating randomly over each coated brownie.
8 to 10 brownies.

HIGH ALTITUDE—Above 3500 Feet: Add ¼ cup flour to dry brownie mix. Bake as directed above.

NUTRIENTS PER 1 BROWNIE

Calories	500	Sodium	230mg
Fat	26g	Potassium	200mg
Cholesterol	25mg		

MIDNIGHT MUNCHERS

LUSCIOUS LAYER BARS

BARS
- 1½ cups firmly packed brown sugar
- ½ cup margarine or butter, softened
- 1½ teaspoons vanilla
- 2 eggs
- 1¾ cups all purpose or unbleached flour
- 2 teaspoons baking powder
  Dash salt
- 2 ounces (2 squares) unsweetened chocolate, melted, cooled

FILLING
- 1 can ready-to-spread coconut pecan frosting

TOPPING
- 1 cup sugar
- 5 tablespoons margarine or butter
- ⅓ cup milk
- 6-ounce package (1 cup) semisweet chocolate chips

Heat oven to 350°F. Grease 13 × 9-inch pan. In large bowl, combine brown sugar and ½ cup margarine; beat until smooth. Add vanilla and eggs; mix well. Lightly spoon flour into measuring cup; level off. Stir in flour, baking powder and salt; blend well. Divide mixture in half; stir chocolate into ½ of mixture.

Drop both mixtures by large tablespoonfuls randomly into greased pan; spread evenly. Bake at 350°F. for 17 to 22 minutes or until golden brown. Cool. Spread filling over bars. Freeze bars for about 30 minutes.

In small saucepan, combine sugar, 5 tablespoons margarine and milk. Bring to a boil. Boil 1 minute, stirring constantly. Remove from heat. Add chocolate chips and stir until melted and smooth. Pour topping over chilled bars. Refrigerate about 30 minutes. Cut into bars. Garnish as desired. Store in refrigerator. **36 bars.**

HIGH ALTITUDE—Above 3500 Feet: No change.

NUTRIENTS PER 1 BAR

Calories	210	Sodium	95mg
Fat	10g	Potassium	90mg
Cholesterol	15mg		

BARS
- 1 package pudding-included German chocolate cake mix
- ½ cup margarine or butter, softened
- ½ cup dairy sour cream
- 3 eggs
- 1 cup chopped nuts
- 2 cups coconut
- 14-ounce can sweetened condensed milk (not evaporated)

FROSTING
- 2½ cups powdered sugar
- 3 tablespoons unsweetened cocoa
- ⅛ teaspoon salt
- 3 tablespoons margarine or butter, softened
- ½ teaspoon vanilla
- 3 to 4 tablespoons milk

Heat oven to 350°F. Grease and flour 15 × 10 × 1-inch baking pan. In large bowl, combine cake mix, ½ cup margarine, sour cream and eggs; beat at low speed until moistened. Beat 2 minutes at highest speed. (Batter will be very thick.) Stir in nuts. Spread in greased and floured pan. Bake at 350°F. for 15 to 18 minutes. *Do not overbake. (Center will puff up and not be firm to touch.)*

In medium bowl, combine coconut and sweetened condensed milk; carefully spoon and spread over partially baked base. Bake an additional 12 to 18 minutes or until light golden brown. Cool slightly.

In small bowl, blend all frosting ingredients, adding 1 tablespoon milk at a time for desired spreading consistency. Beat 2 minutes at medium speed until smooth and creamy. Frost warm bars. Cool completely. Cut into bars.
48 bars.

HIGH ALTITUDE—Above 3500 Feet: No change.

NUTRIENTS PER 1 BAR

Calories	160	Sodium	135mg
Fat	8g	Potassium	80mg
Cholesterol	20mg		

Midnight Munchers

These rich, incredibly delicious bars will satisfy anyone's sweet tooth! We suggest serving them chilled.

Luscious Layer Bars

So easy and so good, this bar is made in a jelly roll pan to yield 48 bars. When you need to serve a crowd, it is a terrific choice.

FROSTED BLOND CASHEW BROWNIES

Frosted Blond Cashew Brownies

Caramel flavor and crunchy cashews permeate this bar. The brownies bake in an 8- or 9-inch pan, the perfect size for a small family.

BROWNIES

1 cup salted cashews
1 cup firmly packed brown sugar
⅓ cup oil
1 teaspoon vanilla
2 eggs
1¼ cups all purpose or unbleached flour
1 teaspoon baking powder
¼ teaspoon salt, if desired

FROSTING

3 ounces (3 squares) white baking bar, cut into pieces
2 tablespoons margarine or butter, softened
2 tablespoons milk
1 cup powdered sugar

Heat oven to 350°F. Grease 8- or 9-inch square pan. Coarsely chop ½ cup of the cashews; set aside. In food processor bowl with metal blade or blender container, process remaining cashews until mixture resembles coarse crumbs; place in medium bowl. Add brown sugar, oil, vanilla and eggs; beat well. Lightly spoon flour into measuring cup; level off. Add flour, baking powder, salt and chopped cashews; blend well. Spread in greased pan. Bake at 350°F. for 20 to 30 minutes or until toothpick inserted in center comes out clean. Cool completely.

In small saucepan over low heat, melt white baking bar, stirring constantly. Remove from heat. Add margarine, milk and powdered sugar; beat until smooth. Frost cooled brownies. Cut into bars. **25 brownies.**

HIGH ALTITUDE—Above 3500 Feet: Decrease brown sugar to ¾ cup; increase flour to 1½ cups. Bake as directed above.

NUTRIENTS PER 1 BROWNIE

Calories	160	Sodium	55mg
Fat	8g	Potassium	85mg
Cholesterol	25mg		

LAYERED SHORTBREAD BARS

1 cup sugar
1 cup margarine or butter, softened
1 egg
2 cups all purpose or unbleached flour
½ to 1 cup finely chopped pecans
¾ cup cherry preserves
½ to 1 cup semi-sweet chocolate chips
1 teaspoon cinnamon

Heat oven to 325°F. Grease and flour 9- or 8-inch square pan. In large bowl, combine sugar, margarine and egg; beat until light and fluffy. Lightly spoon flour into measuring cup; level off. By hand, stir in flour, 1 cup at a time, until well blended. Stir in pecans. Shape dough into ball; divide in half. Wrap half of dough in plastic wrap; refrigerate while preparing bottom layer. Press remaining half of dough evenly in bottom of greased and floured pan. Spread dough with preserves to within ½ inch of edge. Sprinkle with chocolate chips and cinnamon. Roll or pat out remaining half of dough to pan size between sheets of waxed paper. Remove top sheet of waxed paper; invert dough over filling. Press dough lightly onto filling; remove remaining waxed paper. Gently press edges to seal.

Bake at 325°F. for 50 to 60 minutes or until golden brown. Using sharp knife, immediately score top crust into 16 bars. Cool completely. Cut into bars along score lines. **16 bars.**

HIGH ALTITUDE—Above 3500 Feet: No change.

NUTRIENTS PER 1 BAR

Calories	370	Sodium	135mg
Fat	21g	Potassium	100mg
Cholesterol	34mg		

Layered Shortbread Bars

NUT GOODIE BARS

12-ounce package (2 cups) semi-sweet chocolate chips
12-ounce package (2 cups) butterscotch chips
2 cups peanut butter
2 cups salted peanuts
1 cup margarine or butter
½ cup evaporated milk
3⅛-ounce package vanilla pudding and pie filling mix (not instant)
2 pounds (7½ cups) powdered sugar, sifted
1 teaspoon vanilla

Crunchy Snack Bars

Peanut butter and chocolate combine with crisp rice cereal and oats to make a bar treat that brings smiles to the faces of kids of all ages.

Butter 15×10×1-inch baking pan. In large saucepan over low heat, melt chocolate and butterscotch chips, stirring constantly. Remove from heat. Stir in peanut butter, blend well. Spread half of chocolate mixture in buttered pan; refrigerate. Stir peanuts into remaining chocolate mixture; set aside.

Melt margarine in large saucepan over low heat; gradually add evaporated milk. Stir in pudding mix. Cook until mixture is slightly thickened, stirring constantly. *Do not boil.* Remove from heat. Stir in powdered sugar and vanilla; cool slightly. Carefully spread pudding mixture over chilled chocolate layer. Refrigerate 30 minutes. Drop chocolate-peanut mixture by tablespoonfuls over chilled pudding layer; spread gently to cover. Refrigerate until firm; cut into bars. Store tightly covered in refrigerator. **48 bars.**

MICROWAVE DIRECTIONS:
Butter 15×10×1-inch baking pan. In medium microwave-safe bowl, combine chocolate chips and butterscotch chips. Microwave on MEDIUM for 6 to 7 minutes, stirring every 2 minutes. Stir until smooth. Stir in peanut butter; blend well. Spread half of chocolate mixture in buttered pan; refrigerate. Stir peanuts into remaining chocolate mixture; set aside.

Place margarine in large microwave-safe bowl. Microwave on HIGH for 15 to 60 seconds or until melted. Stir in evaporated milk and pudding mix; blend well. Microwave on HIGH for 45 to 60 seconds or until hot. *Do not boil.* Stir in powdered sugar and vanilla.

Carefully spread over chocolate layer. Refrigerate 30 minutes to set. Drop chocolate-peanut mixture by tablespoonfuls over chilled pudding layer; spread gently to cover. Refrigerate until firm; cut into bars. Store tightly covered in refrigerator.

NUTRIENTS PER 1 BAR

Calories	290	Sodium	110mg
Fat	17g	Potassium	160mg
Cholesterol	1mg		

CRUNCHY SNACK BARS

BARS
6-ounce package (1 cup) semi-sweet chocolate chips
½ cup peanut butter chips
⅓ cup margarine
1 teaspoon vanilla
2 cups crisp rice cereal
1 cup quick-cooking rolled oats

GLAZE
¼ cup peanut butter chips
1 teaspoon oil

Grease 9-inch pan. In large saucepan over low heat, melt chocolate chips, ½ cup peanut butter chips and margarine, stirring constantly until smooth. Remove from heat; stir in vanilla. Add cereal and oats; stir until well coated. Press evenly in bottom of greased pan.

In small saucepan over low heat, melt glaze ingredients, stirring constantly until smooth. Drizzle over bars. If desired, refrigerate until set. Cut into bars. **16 bars.**

MICROWAVE DIRECTIONS:
Grease 9-inch pan. In medium microwave-safe bowl, combine chocolate chips, ½ cup peanut butter chips and margarine. Microwave on MEDIUM for 2 to 3 minutes, stirring once halfway through cooking. Stir in vanilla; blend until smooth. Add cereal and oats; stir until well coated. Press evenly in bottom of greased pan.

In small microwave-safe bowl, combine glaze ingredients. Microwave on MEDIUM for 1 to 2 minutes; stir until smooth. Drizzle over bars. If desired, refrigerate until set. Cut into bars.

NUTRIENTS PER 1 BAR

Calories	170	Sodium	105mg
Fat	11g	Potassium	100mg
Cholesterol	0mg		

Orange Cappuccino Bars; Chocolate-Dipped Mandarin Oranges, page 134

ORANGE CAPPUCCINO BARS

BASE
- 1 package pudding-included dark chocolate cake mix
- ½ cup margarine or butter, softened
- 1 egg

FILLING
- 1 envelope unflavored gelatin
- ¼ cup boiling water
- 1 teaspoon instant coffee granules or crystals
- 4 cups powdered sugar
- ¼ cup unsweetened cocoa
- 1 cup margarine or butter, softened
- 2 tablespoons orange-flavored liqueur

TOPPING
- 6-ounce package (1 cup) semi-sweet chocolate chips
- ¼ cup margarine or butter
- 1 teaspoon grated orange peel

Heat oven to 350°F. Grease 15 × 10 × 1-inch baking pan. In large bowl, combine all base ingredients; beat at low speed until crumbly. Press evenly in bottom of greased pan. Bake at 350°F. for 10 minutes. Cool completely.

In another large bowl, dissolve gelatin in boiling water; stir in instant coffee. Add remaining filling ingredients; blend well. Spread filling evenly over cooled base. Refrigerate until set, about 30 minutes.

In small saucepan over low heat, melt chocolate chips and ¼ cup margarine, stirring constantly until smooth. Stir in orange peel. Spoon topping evenly over chilled filling, carefully spreading to cover. Refrigerate until firm. Cut into bars. Store in refrigerator. **48 bars.**

HIGH ALTITUDE — Above 3500 Feet: No change.

NUTRIENTS PER 1 BAR

Calories	160	Sodium	170mg
Fat	9g	Potassium	35mg
Cholesterol	5mg		

Orange Cappuccino Bars

For occasions that call for something exquisite, serve these dark-chocolate, liqueur-laced bars on a doily-lined plate with after dinner coffee.

Clockwise from upper left: Crisp Chocolate Snaps, page 34; Choco-Butterscotch Chip Cookies, page 29; Sour Cream Chocolate Chip Cookies, page 29; Heavenly Chocolate Brownie Cookies, page 33; Sugar Cookie Chipper Slices, page 36

Cookies

The dictionary defines cookie, or cooky, as "a small, usually flat cake made from sweet dough." These words hardly express the pleasures of eating cookies, especially those flavored with chocolate.

Topping off the list of favorites is Chocolate Chip Cookies, of course. In this chapter you'll find a taste-tempting array of cookies inspired by that original recipe—Sour Cream Chocolate Chip Cookies, Choco-Butterscotch Chip Cookies plus Three Chip Cookies combining semi-sweet, milk and white chocolate. And for the chocolate connoisseur who's had it all—Chocolate Macadamia Nut Cookies.

But there's so much more chocolate to enjoy in the realm of cookies. From the sublimely elegant Austrian Torte Cookies to the nostalgic bliss of Chocolate Cherry Cordial Cookies, there are recipes in this chapter to suit every occasion and every chocolate mood. As you browse through this collection, you'll discover that virtually any of your favorite cookies can be made even better with a touch of chocolate. Sugar cookies become Sugar Cookie Chipper Slices. And Christmas spritz dipped in semi-sweet chocolate are transformed into Chocolate Almond Spritz Wafers.

Crispy, buttery, chewy and chocolaty. Cookies are the treats to top off an otherwise ordinary bag lunch, to serve with tea for a pleasant afternoon of conversation with friends or to dazzle diners after a glorious feast in your home.

Many cookies in this collection would make delightful gifts. An assortment of several types, attractively arranged in a box or canister, will make birthdays happier, grandparents jollier and co-workers more mellow.

CHOCOLATE CHIP COOKIES

Through the years, the chocolate chip cookie, with its many taste-tempting variations, has remained America's most popular cookie. For best results, use real chocolate chips to make this chewy, melt-in-your-mouth version.

COOK'S NOTE
Storing Cookies

To keep soft cookies **soft**, store them in a container with a tight-fitting cover. Place sheets of waxed paper between layers so the cookies won't stick together.

To keep crisp cookies **crisp**, store them in a container with a loose-fitting cover if the humidity is low, or a tight-fitting cover if the humidity is high.

¾ cup firmly packed brown sugar
½ cup sugar
½ cup margarine or butter, softened
½ cup shortening
1½ teaspoons vanilla
1 egg
1¾ cups all purpose or unbleached flour
1 teaspoon baking soda
½ teaspoon salt
6-ounce package (1 cup) semi-sweet chocolate chips
½ cup chopped nuts or shelled sunflower seeds, if desired

Heat oven to 375°F. In large bowl, combine brown sugar, sugar, margarine and shortening; beat until light and fluffy. Add vanilla and egg; blend well. Lightly spoon flour into measuring cup; level off. Stir in flour, baking soda and salt; mix well. Stir in chocolate chips and nuts. Drop dough by teaspoonfuls 2 inches apart onto ungreased cookie sheets. Bake at 375°F. for 8 to 10 minutes or until light golden brown. Cool 1 minute; remove from cookie sheets. **4 dozen cookies.**

Chocolate Chip Cookie Bars: Prepare dough as directed in recipe. Spread dough in ungreased 13×9-inch pan. Bake at 375°F. for 15 to 25 minutes or until light golden brown. Cool completely. Cut into bars. **36 bars.**

Chocolate Chip Ice Cream Cookiewiches: Prepare dough as directed in recipe. Drop dough by heaping teaspoonfuls 3 inches apart onto ungreased cookie sheets. Bake at 375°F. for 9 to 14 minutes or until light golden brown. Cool 1 minute; remove from cookie sheets. Cool completely. To assemble each cookiewich, place scoop of favorite flavor ice cream on bottom side of 1 cookie; flatten ice cream slightly. Place another cookie, bottom side down, on top of ice cream. Gently press cookies together in center to form ice cream sandwich. Quickly wrap in foil. Freeze. **12 cookiewiches.**

Chocolate Chocolate Chip Cookies: Prepare dough as directed in recipe, substituting 1 cup margarine or butter, softened, for the ½ cup margarine and ½ cup shortening. Decrease vanilla to 1 teaspoon. Add ¼ cup unsweetened cocoa with flour, baking soda and salt. Drop dough by teaspoonfuls 2 inches apart onto ungreased cookie sheets. Bake at 375°F. for 7 to 11 minutes or until set. **4 dozen cookies.**

Chocolate Chunk Cookies: Prepare dough as directed in recipe, substituting 8 ounces coarsely chopped semi-sweet chocolate for chocolate chips. Drop dough by tablespoonfuls 3 inches apart onto ungreased cookie sheets. Bake at 375°F. for 9 to 12 minutes or until light golden brown. Immediately remove from cookie sheets. **3 dozen cookies.**

Kid-Sized Cookies: Prepare dough as directed in recipe, omitting ½ cup sugar, 1 cup semi-sweet chocolate chips and ½ cup chopped nuts. Increase vanilla to 2 teaspoons. Stir 1 cup candy-coated chocolate pieces and ½ cup shelled sunflower seeds into dough. Refrigerate if necessary for easier handling. Shape dough into 2-inch balls. Place 4 inches apart on ungreased cookie sheets. Press an additional ½ cup candy-coated chocolate pieces into balls to decorate tops of cookies. Bake at 350°F. for 15 to 20 minutes or until light golden brown. Cool 2 minutes; remove from cookie sheets. **14 cookies.**

Maxi Chippers: Prepare dough as directed in recipe. For each cookie, use ⅓ cupful of dough, placing 4 inches apart on ungreased cookie sheets. Bake at 375°F. for 12 to 18 minutes or until light golden brown. Cool 1 minute; remove from cookie sheets. **10 cookies.**

Mini Chippers: Prepare dough as directed in recipe. Drop dough by ½ teaspoonfuls 1 inch apart onto ungreased cookie sheets. Bake at 375°F. for 5 to 7 minutes or until light golden brown. Immediately remove from cookie sheets. **12½ dozen cookies.**

HIGH ALTITUDE—Above 3500 Feet: No change.

NUTRIENTS PER 1 CHOCOLATE CHIP COOKIE

Calories	100	Sodium	70mg
Fat	6g	Potassium	35mg
Cholesterol	6mg		

SOUR CREAM CHOCOLATE CHIP COOKIES

12-ounce package (2 cups) semi-sweet chocolate chips
½ cup sugar
¼ cup firmly packed brown sugar
¾ cup margarine or butter, softened
½ cup dairy sour cream
1 teaspoon vanilla
1 egg
2¼ cups all purpose or unbleached flour
1 teaspoon baking powder
½ teaspoon baking soda

Heat oven to 375°F. In small saucepan over low heat, melt 1 cup of the chocolate chips, stirring constantly until smooth. In large bowl, combine sugar, brown sugar and margarine; beat until light and fluffy. Add sour cream, vanilla, egg and melted chocolate chips; blend well. Lightly spoon flour into measuring cup; level off. Add flour, baking powder and baking soda; blend well. Stir in remaining 1 cup chocolate chips. Drop dough by teaspoonfuls 2 inches apart onto ungreased cookie sheets. Bake at 375°F. for 7 to 10 minutes or until set. Cool 1 minute; remove from cookie sheets. Cool completely. Store tightly covered. **5 dozen cookies.**

HIGH ALTITUDE — Above 3500 Feet: No change.

NUTRIENTS PER 1 COOKIE

Calories	80	Sodium	45mg
Fat	5g	Potassium	30mg
Cholesterol	5mg		

CHOCO-BUTTERSCOTCH CHIP COOKIES

¾ cup sugar
¾ cup firmly packed brown sugar
1 cup shortening
2 teaspoons vanilla
2 eggs
1 cup all purpose or unbleached flour
1 cup whole wheat flour
1 cup wheat germ
1 teaspoon baking powder
1 teaspoon salt
6-ounce package (1 cup) semi-sweet chocolate chips
6-ounce package (1 cup) butterscotch chips

Heat oven to 375°F. Grease cookie sheets. In large bowl, combine sugar, brown sugar and shortening; beat until light and fluffy. Stir in vanilla. Add eggs 1 at a time, beating well after each addition. Lightly spoon flour into measuring cup; level off. Add all purpose flour, whole wheat flour, wheat germ, baking powder and salt; blend well. Stir in chocolate and butterscotch chips. Drop by rounded teaspoonfuls onto greased cookie sheets. Bake at 375°F. for 10 to 12 minutes or until golden brown. **5 dozen cookies.**

HIGH ALTITUDE — Above 3500 Feet: No change.

NUTRIENTS PER 1 COOKIE

Calories	100	Sodium	45mg
Fat	6g	Potassium	40mg
Cholesterol	8mg		

COOK'S NOTE
Softening Brown Sugar

To keep brown sugar moist, store it in a tightly covered container in a cool place. If it does harden, heat it in a 250 to 300°F. oven for a few minutes. Use it immediately, before it hardens again. To soften it in the microwave, bring ½ cup water to a boil. Place the brown sugar in a microwave-safe container near the water. Microwave ½ pound of brown sugar on HIGH for 1½ to 2½ minutes.

CHOCOLATE RAISIN NUT DROPS

Chocolate Raisin Nut Drops

This candylike fudge cookie is easily prepared on the stovetop or in the microwave. For special occasions, the cookies can be made smaller and served in small paper cups.

Chocolate Macadamia Nut Cookies

Chunks of creamy white chocolate and mouth-watering macadamia nuts are scattered throughout these irresistible dark-chocolate cookies. Macadamia nuts are grown commercially in Hawaii. Because of their high fat content, store them tightly covered in a dark, cool place or in the refrigerator.

2 cups sugar
1 cup half-and-half or evaporated milk
½ cup butter
6-ounce package (1 cup) semi-sweet chocolate chips
¾ cup all purpose or unbleached flour
1 cup graham cracker crumbs
1 cup raisins
1 cup chopped toasted almonds*
1 teaspoon vanilla

Grease cookie sheets. In medium saucepan over medium heat, combine sugar, half-and-half and butter. Bring to a full boil, stirring constantly. Boil 10 minutes, stirring occasionally. Remove from heat. Stir in chocolate chips. Lightly spoon flour into measuring cup; level off. Add flour and remaining ingredients; beat well. Let stand 5 minutes. Drop mixture by rounded teaspoonfuls onto greased cookie sheets. Cool completely.
4 dozen cookies.

MICROWAVE DIRECTIONS:
Grease cookie sheets. In 3-quart microwave-safe casserole, combine sugar and half-and-half; blend well. Add butter. Microwave on HIGH for 5 to 6 minutes or until mixture comes to a boil; stir. Microwave on MEDIUM for 10 minutes.** Continue as directed above.

TIPS: *To toast 1 cup almonds, spread on cookie sheet; bake at 375°F. for 5 to 10 minutes or until light golden brown, stirring occasionally. Or, spread in thin layer in microwave-safe pie pan. Microwave on HIGH for 4 to 5 minutes or until light golden brown, stirring occasionally.

**If mixture has a curdled appearance after microwaving, beat with a wire whisk until smooth.

NUTRIENTS PER 1 COOKIE

Calories	110	Sodium	35mg
Fat	5g	Potassium	70mg
Cholesterol	6mg		

CHOCOLATE MACADAMIA NUT COOKIES

¾ cup firmly packed brown sugar
½ cup sugar
1 cup margarine or butter, softened
1 teaspoon almond extract
1 egg
2 cups all purpose or unbleached flour
¼ cup unsweetened cocoa
1 teaspoon baking soda
½ teaspoon salt
6 ounces (6 squares) white baking bar, cut into ½-inch chunks,* or 1 cup vanilla milk chips
3½-ounce jar macadamia nuts, coarsely chopped

Heat oven to 375°F. In large bowl, combine brown sugar, sugar and margarine; beat until light and fluffy. Add almond extract and egg; blend well. Lightly spoon flour into measuring cup; level off. Stir in flour, cocoa, baking soda and salt; blend well. Stir in remaining ingredients. Drop dough by rounded tablespoonsful 2 inches apart onto ungreased cookie sheets. Bake at 375°F. for 8 to 12 minutes or until set. Cool 1 minute; remove from cookie sheets. **2½ to 3 dozen cookies.**

TIP: *If baking bar is difficult to cut, place in microwave-safe bowl and microwave on MEDIUM for 10 seconds.

HIGH ALTITUDE—Above 3500 Feet: Increase flour to 2 cups plus 3 tablespoons. Bake as directed above.

NUTRIENTS PER 1 COOKIE

Calories	150	Sodium	130mg
Fat	9g	Potassium	55mg
Cholesterol	8mg		

Chocolate Macadamia Nut Cookies, page 30; Chocolate Ginger Zebras, page 44

German Chocolate Cake Mix Cookies

GERMAN CHOCOLATE CAKE MIX COOKIES

1 package pudding-included German chocolate cake mix
6-ounce package (1 cup) semi-sweet chocolate chips
½ cup rolled oats
½ cup raisins
½ cup margarine or butter, melted
2 eggs, slightly beaten

Heat oven to 350°F. In large bowl, combine all ingredients; blend well. Drop dough by rounded teaspoonfuls 2 inches apart onto ungreased cookie sheets. Bake at 350°F. for 8 to 10 minutes or until set. Cool 1 minute; remove from cookie sheets. **6 dozen cookies.**

HIGH ALTITUDE – Above 3500 Feet: Add 2 tablespoons flour to dry cake mix. Bake as directed above.

NUTRIENTS PER 1 COOKIE

Calories	60	Sodium	75mg
Fat	3g	Potassium	25mg
Cholesterol	8mg		

German Chocolate Cake Mix Cookies

This recipe was developed for bakers requesting an easy cookie made from a cake mix. The cookies puff up during baking and when cooled after baking contract to form a pretty crinkled top.

CHOCOLATE WALNUT MERINGUES

3 egg whites, room temperature
¼ teaspoon cream of tartar
Dash salt
¾ cup sugar
3 ounces (3 squares) semi-sweet chocolate, melted, cooled
¼ cup ground walnuts

Heat oven to 225°F. Cover cookie sheets with parchment paper. In small bowl, combine egg whites, cream of tartar and salt; beat until soft peaks form. Gradually add sugar; beat until stiff peaks form. Fold in chocolate and walnuts. Drop egg white mixture by teaspoonfuls onto parchment-lined cookie sheets.* Bake at 225°F. for 1½ hours. Cool completely. Remove from parchment paper. Store tightly covered. **4½ dozen cookies.**

NUTRIENTS PER 1 COOKIE

Calories	25	Sodium	5mg
Fat	1g	Potassium	10mg
Cholesterol	0mg		

ORANGE BUTTER COOKIES IN CHOCOLATE

COOKIES
- 1 cup sugar
- ¾ cup butter, softened
- 1 teaspoon vanilla
- 1 egg
- 2 cups all purpose or unbleached flour
- 1 teaspoon baking powder
- ¾ teaspoon salt
- 2 tablespoons grated orange peel

GLAZE
- 6-ounce package (1 cup) semi-sweet chocolate chips
- ¼ cup shortening
- 3 tablespoons light corn syrup

Heat oven to 375°F. In large bowl, combine sugar and butter; beat until light and fluffy. Add vanilla and egg; blend well. Lightly spoon flour into measuring cup; level off. Stir in flour, baking powder, salt and orange peel. Shape dough into 1-inch balls. Place 2 inches apart on ungreased cookie sheets. With bottom of glass dipped in sugar, flatten each ball to ⅛- to ¼-inch thickness. Bake at 375°F. for 6 to 8 minutes or until edges are light golden brown. Cool 1 minute; remove from cookie sheets. Cool completely.

Line cookie sheets with waxed paper. In small saucepan over low heat, combine all glaze ingredients, stirring constantly until melted and smooth. Remove from heat. Set saucepan in hot water to maintain dipping consistency. Dip half of each cookie into glaze; allow excess to drip off. Place dipped cookies on waxed paper-lined cookie sheets. Refrigerate about 10 minutes or until glaze is set. **6 dozen cookies.**

HIGH ALTITUDE — Above 3500 Feet: No change.

NUTRIENTS PER 1 COOKIE

Calories	70	Sodium	50mg
Fat	4g	Potassium	15mg
Cholesterol	8mg		

HEAVENLY CHOCOLATE BROWNIE COOKIES

- 4 ounces (4 squares) semi-sweet chocolate, chopped
- 2 ounces (2 squares) unsweetened chocolate, chopped
- ⅓ cup margarine or butter
- ¾ cup sugar
- 1½ teaspoons instant coffee granules or crystals
- 2 eggs
- ½ cup all purpose or unbleached flour
- ¼ teaspoon baking powder
- ¼ teaspoon salt
- ¾ cup milk chocolate chips
- ¾ cup chopped walnuts

Heat oven to 350°F. Line cookie sheets with parchment or brown paper. In small saucepan over low heat, melt semi-sweet chocolate, unsweetened chocolate and margarine, stirring constantly until smooth. Remove from heat; cool.

In large bowl, combine sugar, instant coffee and eggs; beat at high speed 2 to 3 minutes. Add melted chocolate; blend well. Lightly spoon flour into measuring cup; level off. Stir in flour, baking powder and salt; blend well. Stir in milk chocolate chips and walnuts; mix well.

Drop dough by teaspoonfuls 2 inches apart onto parchment-paper-lined cookie sheets. Bake at 350°F. for 7 to 11 minutes or until tops of cookies are cracked. *Do not overbake.* Cool 1 minute; remove from parchment paper. **3 dozen cookies.**

HIGH ALTITUDE — Above 3500 Feet: No change.

NUTRIENTS PER 1 COOKIE

Calories	110	Sodium	40mg
Fat	7g	Potassium	55mg
Cholesterol	15mg		

Orange Butter Cookies in Chocolate

These tender chocolate-dipped cookies will melt in your mouth. Store the cookies in a covered container with waxed paper between the layers.

Heavenly Chocolate Brownie Cookies

This is probably one of the best little cookies you'll ever eat. Parchment paper, used in this recipe to minimize sticking, is readily available at supermarkets or specialty food stores.

CRISP CHOCOLATE SNAPS

CLOVERLEAF COOKIES

Crisp Chocolate Snaps

Chocolate lovers will find this eye-catching cookie irresistible. Smaller-sized snaps can be made for party trays.

COOK'S NOTE
Baking Cookies

To avoid excess spreading, grease cookie sheets only if the recipe calls for it. Cool cookie sheets between bakings. Hot cookie sheets can cause the fat in the dough to melt before baking, resulting in flatter cookies. Wipe cookie sheets with paper towels between bakings if necessary to remove crumbs.

---

2 cups sugar
1 cup firmly packed brown sugar
1½ cups margarine or butter, softened
2 teaspoons vanilla
½ teaspoon red food coloring, if desired
3 eggs
6 ounces (6 squares) unsweetened chocolate, melted, cooled
4 cups all purpose or unbleached flour
2 teaspoons baking soda
1 teaspoon salt
Sugar

In large bowl, combine 2 cups sugar, brown sugar and margarine; beat until light and fluffy. Add vanilla, food coloring, eggs and unsweetened chocolate; blend well. Lightly spoon flour into measuring cup; level off. Stir in flour, baking soda and salt; blend well. Refrigerate dough up to 24 hours for easier handling.

Heat oven to 350°F. Lightly grease cookie sheets. Shape dough into 1½-inch balls; roll in sugar. Place 3 inches apart on greased cookie sheets. Bake at 350°F. for 8 to 12 minutes or until set. (Cookies will puff up and then flatten.) Cool 1 minute; remove from cookie sheets.

6 dozen cookies.

HIGH ALTITUDE – Above 3500 Feet: No change.

NUTRIENTS PER 1 COOKIE

Calories	110	Sodium	110mg
Fat	5g	Potassium	45mg
Cholesterol	10mg		

¾ cup firmly packed brown sugar
½ cup sugar
½ cup margarine or butter, softened
½ cup shortening
1½ teaspoons vanilla
1 egg
1¾ cups all purpose or unbleached flour
1 teaspoon baking soda
½ teaspoon salt
½ cup miniature semi-sweet chocolate chips
¼ cup chunky peanut butter
1 ounce (1 square) unsweetened chocolate, melted, cooled

In large bowl, combine brown sugar, sugar, margarine and shortening; beat until light and fluffy. Add vanilla and egg; blend well. Lightly spoon flour into measuring cup; level off. Stir in flour, baking soda and salt; blend well. Divide dough into 3 equal portions; place each in small bowl. Add chocolate chips to first portion, peanut butter to second and chocolate to third; blend each well. Refrigerate dough ½ hour for easier handling.

Heat oven to 375°F. Shape ½ teaspoonful of each dough into ball. To form cookie, place 1 ball of each flavor dough cloverleaf-style on ungreased cookie sheet. Repeat with remaining dough. Bake at 375°F. for 10 to 12 minutes or until set. Cool 1 minute; carefully remove from cookie sheet.

3½ dozen cookies.

HIGH ALTITUDE – Above 3500 Feet: No change.

NUTRIENTS PER 1 COOKIE

Calories	110	Sodium	90mg
Fat	7g	Potassium	45mg
Cholesterol	5mg		

Cloverleaf Cookies

SNAPPY TURTLE COOKIES

COOKIES

½ cup firmly packed brown sugar
½ cup margarine or butter, softened
¼ teaspoon vanilla
⅛ teaspoon maple flavor, if desired
1 egg
1 egg, separated
1½ cups all purpose or unbleached flour
¼ teaspoon baking soda
¼ teaspoon salt
1½ to 2 cups split pecan halves

FROSTING

⅓ cup semi-sweet chocolate chips
3 tablespoons milk
1 tablespoon margarine or butter
1 cup powdered sugar

In medium bowl, combine brown sugar and ½ cup margarine; beat until light and fluffy. Add vanilla, maple flavor, 1 whole egg and 1 egg yolk; beat well. Lightly spoon flour into measuring cup; level off. Stir in flour, baking soda and salt; mix well. Refrigerate dough for easier handling.

Heat oven to 350°F. Grease cookie sheets. Arrange pecan pieces in groups of 5 on greased cookie sheets to resemble head and legs of turtle. In small bowl, beat egg white. Shape rounded teaspoonfuls of dough into balls. Dip bottoms in beaten egg white, press lightly onto pecans. (Tips of pecans should show.) Bake at 350°F. for 10 to 12 minutes or until light golden brown around edges. *Do not overbake.* Immediately remove from cookie sheets. Cool.

In small saucepan over low heat, melt chocolate chips with milk and 1 tablespoon margarine, stirring constantly until smooth. Remove from heat; stir in powdered sugar. Add additional powdered sugar if necessary for desired spreading consistency. Frost cookies. **3½ dozen cookies.**

Sugar Cookie Chipper Slices

The dough for this "big batch" recipe is shaped into rolls and frozen for easier slicing. Bake half to enjoy now and freeze the rest for later.

HIGH ALTITUDE—Above 3500 Feet: No change.

NUTRIENTS PER 1 COOKIE

Calories	110	Sodium	50mg
Fat	7g	Potassium	45mg
Cholesterol	10mg		

SUGAR COOKIE CHIPPER SLICES

1 cup sugar
1 cup margarine or butter, softened
½ teaspoon almond extract
2 eggs
2 cups all purpose or unbleached flour
¾ cup whole wheat flour
1 teaspoon baking soda
12-ounce package (2 cups) miniature semi-sweet chocolate chips

In large bowl, combine sugar and margarine; beat until light and fluffy. Add almond extract and eggs; blend well. Lightly spoon flour into measuring cup; level off. Add all purpose flour, whole wheat flour and baking soda; blend well. Stir in chocolate chips. Refrigerate 2 hours. Divide dough into 4 equal portions. Shape each portion into roll 1½ inches in diameter. Wrap each roll in waxed paper. Freeze 1½ hours or until firm.

Heat oven to 350°F. Cut dough into ¼-inch slices. Place 1 inch apart on ungreased cookie sheets. Bake at 350°F. for 8 to 10 minutes or until edges are very light golden brown. Cool 1 minute; remove from cookie sheets. Cool completely. **6 dozen cookies.**

HIGH ALTITUDE—Above 3500 Feet: Increase whole wheat flour to 1 cup. Bake as directed above.

NUTRIENTS PER 1 COOKIE

Calories	80	Sodium	45mg
Fat	4g	Potassium	25mg
Cholesterol	8mg		

Chocolate Cherry Cordial Cookies

CHOCOLATE CHERRY CORDIAL COOKIES

COOKIES

- ½ cup semi-sweet chocolate chips
- ½ cup firmly packed brown sugar
- ¼ cup margarine or butter, softened
- 1 egg
- 1 cup all purpose or unbleached flour
- ½ teaspoon baking powder
- 16-ounce jar maraschino cherries, well drained, reserving 2 to 3 teaspoons liquid

FROSTING

- ½ cup semi-sweet chocolate chips
- 2 teaspoons margarine or butter
  Reserved 2 to 3 teaspoons maraschino cherry liquid

In small saucepan over low heat, melt ½ cup chocolate chips, stirring constantly until smooth. In small bowl, combine brown sugar and ¼ cup margarine; beat until light and fluffy. Add egg and melted chocolate chips; blend well. Lightly spoon flour into measuring cup; level off. Stir in flour and baking powder; blend well. Refrigerate dough 10 to 15 minutes for easier handling.

Heat oven to 350°F. Wrap 1 teaspoonful dough evenly around each cherry to completely cover. Place 1 inch apart on ungreased cookie sheets. Bake at 350°F. for 10 to 14 minutes or until set. Remove from cookie sheets. Cool completely.

Line cookie sheets with waxed paper. In small saucepan over low heat, melt ½ cup chocolate chips and 2 teaspoons margarine, stirring constantly until smooth. Add reserved maraschino cherry liquid 1 teaspoon at a time for desired dipping consistency. Dip tops of cooled· cookies in frosting. Place dipped cookies on waxed paper-lined cookie sheets. Allow frosting to set.
4 dozen cookies.

HIGH ALTITUDE – Above 3500 Feet: Increase flour to 1¼ cups. Bake as directed above.

NUTRIENTS PER 1 COOKIE

Calories	60	Sodium	20mg
Fat	3g	Potassium	25mg
Cholesterol	6mg		

Chocolate Cherry Cordial Cookies

This is a delicious cookie version of the ever-popular chocolate-covered cherry. The recipe makes four dozen — plenty of cookies to enjoy and some to keep on hand in the freezer.

THREE CHIP COOKIES

Three Chip Cookies

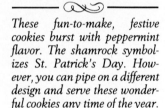

In this recipe, semi-sweet, milk and white chocolate are added to a traditionally flavored cookie dough. It's an old favorite with some new surprises!

Chocolate Peppermint Shamrock Cookies

These fun-to-make, festive cookies burst with peppermint flavor. The shamrock symbolizes St. Patrick's Day. However, you can pipe on a different design and serve these wonderful cookies any time of the year.

¾ cup sugar
¾ cup firmly packed brown sugar
½ cup shortening
½ cup margarine or butter, softened
2 teaspoons vanilla
2 eggs
2½ cups all purpose or unbleached flour
1 teaspoon baking soda
½ teaspoon salt
¾ cup semi-sweet chocolate chips
¾ cup milk chocolate chips
¾ cup vanilla milk chips or 4 ounces (4 squares) white baking bar, cut into pieces

In large bowl, combine sugar, brown sugar, shortening and margarine; beat until light and fluffy. Add vanilla and eggs; blend well. Lightly spoon flour into measuring cup; level off. Add flour, baking soda and salt; blend well. Stir in all of the chips. Refrigerate 1 hour for easier handling.

Heat oven to 375°F. Shape dough into 1½-inch balls. Place 2 inches apart on ungreased cookie sheets. With bottom of glass dipped in sugar, flatten each ball slightly. Bake at 375°F. for 8 to 10 minutes or until golden brown. Cool 1 minute; remove from cookie sheets.
3 dozen cookies.

HIGH ALTITUDE – Above 3500 Feet: Increase flour to 3 cups. Bake as directed above.

NUTRIENTS PER 1 COOKIE

Calories	180	Sodium	105mg
Fat	9g	Potassium	65mg
Cholesterol	15mg		

CHOCOLATE PEPPERMINT SHAMROCK COOKIES

COOKIES
1 cup sugar
½ cup shortening
½ teaspoon peppermint extract
3 ounces (3 squares) unsweetened chocolate, melted
2 eggs
1¾ cups all purpose or unbleached flour
¾ teaspoon baking soda
½ teaspoon salt
Sugar

TOPPING
½ cup all purpose or unbleached flour
½ cup margarine or butter, softened
1 tablespoon warm water
4 drops green food coloring

In large bowl, combine 1 cup sugar and shortening; beat until light and fluffy. Add peppermint extract, chocolate and eggs; blend well. Lightly spoon flour into measuring cup; level off. Stir in 1¾ cups flour, baking soda and salt; blend well. Shape dough into 1-inch balls; roll in sugar. Place 2 inches apart on ungreased cookie sheets. Flatten each ball with bottom of glass dipped in sugar.

Heat oven to 375°F. Lightly spoon flour into measuring cup; level off. In small bowl, combine ½ cup flour, margarine and water; blend well. Stir in food coloring. Spoon mixture into pastry bag with small writing tip. Pipe shamrock design on top of each cookie. Bake at 375°F. for 6 to 10 minutes or until set.
6 to 6½ dozen cookies.

HIGH ALTITUDE – Above 3500 Feet: Increase flour in cookies to 1¾ cups plus 1 tablespoon. Bake as directed above.

NUTRIENTS PER 1 COOKIE

Calories	60	Sodium	40mg
Fat	3g	Potassium	15mg
Cholesterol	6mg		

LEMON-FILLED CHOCOLATE THUMBPRINTS

COOKIES
½ cup sugar
½ cup margarine or butter, softened
½ teaspoon vanilla
2 ounces (2 squares) semi-sweet chocolate, melted, cooled
1 egg yolk
1 cup all purpose or unbleached flour
½ cup finely ground almonds

FILLING
½ cup sugar
1 teaspoon cornstarch
Dash salt
2 tablespoons lemon juice
2 teaspoons margarine or butter
1 egg, slightly beaten
¼ teaspoon grated lemon peel

In large bowl, combine ½ cup sugar and ½ cup margarine; beat until light and fluffy. Add vanilla, chocolate and egg yolk; blend well. Lightly spoon flour into measuring cup; level off. Stir in flour and almonds; blend well. Refrigerate dough ½ hour for easier handling.

In medium saucepan, combine all filling ingredients except lemon peel. Cook over low heat 10 to 15 minutes or until smooth and thickened, stirring constantly. Remove from heat; stir in lemon peel. Cool slightly.

Heat oven to 375°F. Shape dough into 1-inch balls. Place 2 inches apart on ungreased cookie sheets. With thumb or handle of wooden spoon, make imprint in center of each cookie. Bake at 375°F. for 8 to 10 minutes or until set. Remove from oven and make imprint again. Cool 1 minute; remove from cookie sheets. Spoon ½ teaspoonful of filling into center of each cookie.
2½ dozen cookies.

HIGH ALTITUDE – Above 3500 Feet: No change.

NUTRIENTS PER 1 COOKIE
Calories	90	Sodium	45mg
Fat	5g	Potassium	30mg
Cholesterol	20mg		

KAHLUA BUTTERCREAM-FILLED COOKIE CUPS

COOKIE CUPS
⅓ cup sugar
½ cup butter, softened
½ teaspoon vanilla
⅛ teaspoon almond extract
1 egg yolk
1 cup all purpose or unbleached flour
Dash salt

FILLING
2 tablespoons unsweetened cocoa
½ cup butter, softened
1 cup powdered sugar
2 tablespoons coffee-flavored liqueur
Grated Chocolate (See Index)

Grease 24 miniature muffin cups or 1½-inch tartlet tins. In small bowl, combine sugar and ½ cup butter; beat until light and fluffy. Add vanilla, almond extract and egg yolk; blend well. Lightly spoon flour into measuring cup; level off. Stir in flour and salt; blend well. Refrigerate dough 1 hour for easier handling.

Heat oven to 350°F. Place about 2 teaspoonfuls dough into each greased muffin cup. Press dough in bottom and up sides. Bake at 350°F. for 10 to 15 minutes or until light golden brown. Very carefully remove from muffin cups. Cool completely.

In small bowl, combine cocoa and ½ cup butter; beat until light and fluffy. Add powdered sugar and liqueur; blend well. Spoon or pipe filling into cookie cups. Sprinkle filling with grated chocolate. Store in refrigerator.
2 dozen cookie cups.

HIGH ALTITUDE – Above 3500 Feet: Decrease butter in cookie cups to 7 tablespoons. Bake as directed above.

NUTRIENTS PER 1 COOKIE CUP
Calories	130	Sodium	85mg
Fat	8g	Potassium	15mg
Cholesterol	30mg		

Kahlua Buttercream-Filled Cookie Cups

This recipe is especially attractive when the cups are made in tartlet tins. Use tins of various shapes to create an intriguing tray of cookies that will entice each and every guest.

COOK'S NOTE
Shortening for Cookie Making

The type of shortening or fat used will affect the quality and flavor of cookies. Butter and margarine give rich flavor and crisp texture to cookies. Vegetable shortening adds little flavor and results in a crunchier, more crumbly cookie. Diet or whipped margarines are not recommended for baking because their lower fat content gives unsatisfactory results.

Strawberry Cream Horns

STRAWBERRY CREAM HORNS

COOKIE CONES
1 egg
½ cup sugar
¼ cup margarine or butter, melted
1 teaspoon almond extract
⅔ cup all purpose or unbleached flour
⅛ teaspoon salt
⅓ cup milk

FILLING
4-ounce bar sweet cooking chocolate, melted
1 cup sliced strawberries or whole raspberries
2 tablespoons powdered sugar
1½ cups whipping cream, whipped
⅛ teaspoon almond extract
Grated Chocolate, if desired (See Index)

Strawberry Cream Horns

These pretty dessert cookies are perfect for a special occasion. If desired, the cookie cones can be made up to twenty-four hours in advance and stored in an airtight container at room temperature. Fill them with the whipped cream mixture just before they are served.

In medium bowl, beat egg slightly. Add sugar, margarine and almond extract; blend well. Lightly spoon flour into measuring cup; level off. Stir in flour and salt. Add milk; blend well.

Heat ungreased, non-stick surface electric skillet or crepe pan to 350°F. (medium-high heat). Spoon scant tablespoonful of batter into skillet; quickly spread to 3-inch circle.* Cook about 1 minute or until deep golden brown. Turn and cook other side for 1 minute or until deep golden brown. Remove from skillet; immediately wrap around cone-shaped form, making sure bottom is closed.** Allow cone to cool. (Cone will harden and maintain its shape as it cools.) Remove cookie cone from cone-shaped form; cool completely. Repeat with remaining batter. Cones can be made ahead and stored in an airtight container at room temperature.

Brush insides of cooled cookie cones with melted chocolate. Refrigerate until chocolate is set. In blender container, puree strawberries. Stir in powdered sugar. Fold in whipped cream and almond extract. Spoon or pipe into cones. Sprinkle filling with grated chocolate. Serve immediately.

3 dozen cookies.

TIPS: *If batter is too thick to spread, add 1 to 2 tablespoons additional milk.

**To make a cone-shaped form, wrap foil around purchased sugar cone or shape several layers of foil into cone shape.

HIGH ALTITUDE — Above 3500 Feet: No change.

NUTRIENTS PER 1 COOKIE

Calories	90	Sodium	30mg
Fat	7g	Potassium	40mg
Cholesterol	22mg		

TRIPLE CHOCOLATE STRIP COOKIES

COOKIES
  2 cups all purpose or unbleached flour
  ½ cup unsweetened cocoa
  ½ teaspoon baking soda
  ¼ teaspoon salt
  ¾ cup sugar
  ½ cup firmly packed brown sugar
  ¾ cup margarine or butter, softened
  2 eggs
  12-ounce package (2 cups) semi-sweet chocolate chips

GLAZES
  2 ounces (2 squares) white baking bar or vanilla-flavored candy coating
  2 ounces (2 squares) semi-sweet chocolate, cut into pieces
  ½ teaspoon margarine or butter

Heat oven to 350°F. Lightly grease 2 cookie sheets. Lightly spoon flour into measuring cup; level off. In medium bowl, combine flour, cocoa, baking soda and salt; set aside. In large bowl, combine sugar, brown sugar and margarine; beat until light and fluffy. Add eggs; blend well. Stir in flour mixture; blend well. Stir in chocolate chips. Divide dough into 4 equal portions. Shape each portion into 12 × 1½-inch roll. Place 2 rolls 2 inches apart on each greased cookie sheet. Bake at 350°F. for 14 to 18 minutes or until toothpick inserted in center of each roll comes out almost clean. Remove from cookie sheets; cool on wire rack 10 minutes.

In small heavy saucepan over low heat, melt white baking bar, stirring constantly until smooth. Drizzle over 2 of the cooled rolls. In same saucepan, melt semi-sweet chocolate and margarine, stirring constantly until smooth. Drizzle over remaining 2 cooled rolls. Allow glazes to set. Cut rolls diagonally into 1-inch-wide strips. **4 dozen cookies.**

HIGH ALTITUDE -- Above 3500 Feet: No change.

NUTRIENTS PER 1 COOKIE

Calories	130	Sodium	65mg
Fat	7g	Potassium	55mg
Cholesterol	10mg		

MANDARIN ORANGE TRUFFLE COOKIES

  11-ounce can mandarin orange segments, drained
  6-ounce package (1 cup) semi-sweet chocolate chips
  ¼ cup whipping cream or evaporated milk
  3 tablespoons butter
  12-ounce box vanilla wafers, crushed (3 cups)
  ½ cup powdered sugar
  ½ cup ground almonds
  2 tablespoons orange-flavored liqueur
  ¾ cup chocolate-flavored sprinkles

In blender container or food processor bowl with metal blade, chop oranges very fine. In heavy saucepan, combine oranges, chocolate chips, whipping cream and butter. Cook over low heat until chocolate melts, stirring constantly. Cook an additional 5 minutes, stirring occasionally. Stir in vanilla wafer crumbs, sugar, almonds and liqueur. Refrigerate dough 30 minutes for easier handling. Shape dough into 1-inch balls; roll in chocolate sprinkles. Store in tightly covered container in refrigerator. **4½ dozen cookies.**

MICROWAVE DIRECTIONS:
Chop oranges as directed above. In medium microwave-safe bowl, combine oranges, chocolate chips, whipping cream and butter. Microwave on HIGH for 3 minutes or until chocolate melts, stirring twice during cooking. Continue as directed above.

NUTRIENTS PER 1 COOKIE

Calories	70	Sodium	25mg
Fat	4g	Potassium	30mg
Cholesterol	6mg		

Triple Chocolate Strip Cookies

Make dozens of chocolate cookies in a snap by baking the rich chocolate dough in logs and then cutting them into strips.

Mandarin Orange Truffle Cookies

A cookie-candy combination, this easy-to-make treat has a delicate, rich flavor without being overly sweet. Serve the cookies in colored foil candy papers for a special touch.

AUSTRIAN TORTE COOKIES

CHOCOLATE VALENTINE COOKIES

Austrian Torte Cookies

These fancy rolled cookies feature an apricot filling and a chocolate glaze. For easier handling, roll the dough between sheets of waxed paper.

Chocolate Valentine Cookies

Bake a batch of these special heart-shaped, cherry-filled chocolate cookies for a special Valentine. For a unique gift or centerpiece, make a beautiful long-stemmed cookie bouquet as described in the recipe.

COOKIES
- 1 cup butter or margarine, softened
- 1 cup sugar
- 3 tablespoons milk
- 1 teaspoon vanilla
- ½ teaspoon grated lemon peel
- 1 egg
- 3 cups all purpose or unbleached flour
- 1½ teaspoons baking powder
- ½ teaspoon salt

FILLING
- 1 cup apricot preserves

GLAZE
- 2 ounces (2 squares) semi-sweet chocolate
- 1 tablespoon shortening

Heat oven to 400°F. In large bowl, combine butter and sugar; beat until light and fluffy. Add milk, vanilla, lemon peel and egg; blend well. Lightly spoon flour into measuring cup; level off. Stir in flour, baking powder and salt; blend well. Refrigerate dough 1 hour for easier handling. On lightly floured surface, roll dough ⅓ at a time to ⅛-inch thickness. Using floured 2-inch and 1½-inch fluted cookie cutters, cut equal number of cookies with each cutter. Place 2 inches apart on ungreased cookie sheets. Bake at 400°F. for 5 to 8 minutes or until edges are light golden brown. Cool 1 minute; remove from cookie sheets.

To assemble, spread ½ teaspoonful of the preserves over bottom of 1½-inch cookie; place preserve side down on top of 2-inch cookie. Repeat with remaining cookies. In small saucepan over low heat, melt chocolate with shortening, stirring constantly until smooth. Drizzle glaze over assembled cookies.
6 dozen sandwich cookies.

HIGH ALTITUDE – Above 3500 Feet: No change.

NUTRIENTS PER 1 SANDWICH COOKIE

Calories	70	Sodium	50mg
Fat	3g	Potassium	15mg
Cholesterol	11mg		

COOKIES
- 1 cup sugar
- 1 cup margarine or butter, softened
- ¼ cup milk
- 1 teaspoon vanilla
- 1 egg
- 2¾ cups all purpose or unbleached flour
- ½ cup unsweetened cocoa
- ¾ teaspoon baking powder
- ¼ teaspoon baking soda

FROSTING
- 2 cups powdered sugar
- ½ cup margarine or butter, softened
- Red food coloring
- 2 or 3 tablespoons maraschino cherry liquid or milk

In large bowl, combine sugar and 1 cup margarine; beat until light and fluffy. Add milk, vanilla and egg; blend well. Lightly spoon flour into measuring cup; level off. Stir in flour, cocoa, baking powder and baking soda; blend well. Refrigerate 1 hour for easier handling.

Heat oven to 350°F. On floured surface, roll ⅓ of dough to ⅛-inch thickness. (Keep remaining dough in refrigerator until used.) Cut with floured 2½-inch heart-shaped cookie cutter. Place half of cookies 1 inch apart on ungreased cookie sheets. Cut 1-inch heart shape from center of remaining cookies. Remove centers; combine with remaining dough and refrigerate before re-rolling. Place cut-out cookies on ungreased cookie sheets. Repeat with remaining dough. Bake at 350°F. for 9 to 11 minutes or until set. Immediately remove from cookie sheets. Cool completely.

In small bowl, combine all frosting ingredients, adding cherry liquid 1 tablespoon at a time for desired spreading consistency. To assemble, frost bottom sides of whole cookies. Top each with cut-out cookie.
4 dozen sandwich cookies.

Chocolate Valentine Heart Bouquet

Chocolate Valentine Heart Bouquet: Bake cookies as directed above. Prepare frosting as directed above. Frost bottom sides of whole cookies. Press about 1½ inches of a 12-inch wooden skewer "stem" into frosting on whole cookie. If necessary, spread additional frosting to cover skewer. Top with cut-out cookie. Refrigerate on cookie sheets for about 1 hour to set frosting. Messages or designs can be added with decorator icing. Arrange bouquet in vase; add roses and baby's breath, if desired.

HIGH ALTITUDE – Above 3500 Feet: Decrease baking powder to ¼ teaspoon. Bake as directed above.

NUTRIENTS PER 1 SANDWICH COOKIE

Calories	110	Sodium	85mg
Fat	6g	Potassium	20mg
Cholesterol	6mg		

DOMINO COOKIES

CHOCOLATE GINGER ZEBRAS

Domino Cookies

This rich chocolate shortbread is carefully scored and decorated with vanilla milk chips to resemble dominoes. They will simply melt in your mouth.

Chocolate Ginger Zebras

"Sugar and spice and everything nice" are baked into these crisp chocolate cookies that have a white chocolate drizzle.

1 cup powdered sugar
1 cup margarine or butter, softened
1 teaspoon vanilla
2 cups all purpose or unbleached flour
¼ cup unsweetened cocoa
Vanilla milk chips

Heat oven to 325°F. In large bowl, combine powdered sugar and margarine; beat until light and fluffy. Add vanilla; blend well. Lightly spoon flour into measuring cup; level off. Stir in flour and cocoa; blend well. Press dough out to 12×6-inch rectangle on ungreased cookie sheet. Using knife, score 5 lengthwise lines 1 inch apart and 11 crosswise lines 1 inch apart in dough, to make rectangle shapes. Arrange vanilla milk chips flat side up inside score lines to resemble dots on dominoes. (Two squares will equal 1 domino cookie.) Bake at 325°F. for 20 to 23 minutes or until slightly firm to the touch. Immediately cut along score lines into 2×1-inch rectangles. Cool 5 minutes; remove from cookie sheet. **3 dozen cookies.**

HIGH ALTITUDE – Above 3500 Feet: No change.

NUTRIENTS PER 1 COOKIE

Calories	100	Sodium	65mg
Fat	6g	Potassium	20mg
Cholesterol	0mg		

COOKIES
¼ cup sugar
⅓ cup shortening
¼ cup unsweetened cocoa
¼ cup dark corn syrup
2 tablespoons milk
1 egg
1½ cups all purpose or unbleached flour
½ teaspoon baking soda
½ teaspoon baking powder
½ teaspoon ginger
½ teaspoon cinnamon
⅛ teaspoon cloves

GLAZE
3 ounces vanilla-flavored candy coating
2 tablespoons shortening

In large bowl, combine sugar and ⅓ cup shortening; beat until light and fluffy. Add cocoa, corn syrup, milk and egg; blend well. Lightly spoon flour into measuring cup; level off. Stir in flour, baking soda, baking powder, ginger, cinnamon and cloves; blend well. Refrigerate dough 1½ to 2 hours for easier handling.

Heat oven to 350°F. Lightly grease cookie sheets. On floured surface, roll dough to ⅛-inch thickness. Cut with floured 2½- to 3-inch cookie cutter. Place 1 inch apart on greased cookie sheets. Bake at 350°F. for 6 to 9 minutes or until set. Immediately remove from cookie sheets. Cool completely.

In small saucepan over low heat, melt candy coating and 2 tablespoons shortening, stirring constantly until smooth. Drizzle over cooled cookies. Allow to set. **2½ to 3 dozen cookies.**

HIGH ALTITUDE – Above 3500 Feet: Increase flour to 1½ cups plus 1 tablespoon. Bake as directed above.

NUTRIENTS PER 1 COOKIE

Calories	70	Sodium	30mg
Fat	3g	Potassium	15mg
Cholesterol	8mg		

Chocolate Almond Spritz Wafers

CHOCOLATE ALMOND SPRITZ WAFERS

COOKIES
- 1 cup powdered sugar
- 1 cup margarine or butter, softened
- 1 teaspoon almond extract
- 1 egg
- 2⅓ cups all purpose or unbleached flour
- ½ teaspoon salt

GLAZE
- 8 ounces (8 squares) semi-sweet chocolate, cut into pieces
- 2 tablespoons shortening
- Almond slices

Heat oven to 400°F. In large bowl, combine powdered sugar and margarine; beat until light and fluffy. Add almond extract and egg; blend well. Lightly spoon flour into measuring cup; level off. Stir in flour and salt; blend well. Spoon dough into cookie press fitted with bar plate. Form 4 strips of dough the length of an ungreased cookie sheet. Score the cookie dough crosswise at 2½-inch intervals. Bake at 400°F. for 3 to 5 minutes or until set but not brown. Cut strips into individual cookies on scored lines. Immediately remove from cookie sheet. Cool completely.

Line cookie sheets with waxed paper. In small saucepan over low heat, melt chocolate and shortening, stirring constantly until smooth. Remove from heat. Set saucepan in hot water to maintain dipping consistency. Dip half of cooled cookie into glaze; allow excess to drip off. Place dipped cookie on waxed-paper-lined cookie sheets. Sprinkle or arrange almond slices over chocolate. Repeat with remaining cookies. Allow glaze to set. Store between sheets of waxed paper in loosely covered container in cool place.
8 dozen cookies.

HIGH ALTITUDE—Above 3500 Feet: No change.

NUTRIENTS PER 1 COOKIE

Calories	50	Sodium	35mg
Fat	3g	Potassium	15mg
Cholesterol	2mg		

Starlight Double-Delight Cake, page 48; White Chocolate Roses, page 129; Chocolate Curls, page 128; Chocolate Leaves, page 126

Cakes, Tortes & Frostings

Cake is the crowning glory of a fine meal. It's a symbol of celebration. And it can be a simple yet sincere way to welcome guests into your home. Whatever the occasion, you'll find a recipe in this chapter that's sure to make it a special event. Many are very easy to do, calling for one-bowl scratch preparation or using cake mixes for convenience.

When your occasion calls for a truly grand finale, try one of the torte recipes in this collection, such as Dark Chocolate Sacher Torte, an adaptation of a famous Viennese dessert. But don't be intimidated by the name. Think of a torte as a specially dressed layer cake with two to four layers and filling between the layers. Although glamorous in appearance and taste, tortes can be very easy to prepare, as you will learn when you use these recipes.

For more casual gatherings, there are chocolaty versions of cakes remembered from family reunions and potluck suppers. Chocolate Pound Cake is a moist and tender cake, topped with a rich chocolate glaze. Another favorite for toting to picnics or for casual entertaining is the easy-to-prepare Chocolate Banana Snack Cake.

There's "magic" in this collection, too. As Hot Fudge Pudding Cake bakes, a moist and tender cake layer forms atop a chocolate-rich layer of pudding. And Upside-Down German Chocolate Cake starts with the frosting on the bottom of the baking pan.

To finish off your chocolate creations, we have included equally tempting chocolate frostings. Spread White Buttercream Frosting on Delicious Devil's Food Cake. Team creamy Cocoa-Lite Frosting with Double Chocolate Chunk Cupcakes. Or create your own combinations with these frostings. All are scrumptious ways to dress up your very best cakes and tortes.

STARLIGHT DOUBLE-DELIGHT CAKE

Starlight Double-Delight Cake

Light peppermint flavor highlights this luscious layer cake. Though the method is a bit unusual, it is very easy to prepare. Originally a winner in the 3rd Bake-Off® contest, it is enjoying renewed popularity and now ranks as our second most often requested recipe.

COOK'S NOTE
Storing Cakes

Unfrosted cakes left in the baking pan are easily stored by covering the pan with its own lid or with a tight covering of foil or plastic wrap.

Frosted layer and **tube cakes** retain moisture and attractive appearance when stored under a cake cover or similar device that keeps out air without touching the frosting.

FROSTING
2 (3-ounce) packages cream cheese, softened
½ cup margarine or butter, softened
½ teaspoon vanilla
½ teaspoon peppermint extract
6 cups (1½ pounds) powdered sugar
¼ cup water heated to 115° to 120°F.
4 ounces (4 squares) semi-sweet chocolate, melted

CAKE
2 cups frosting mixture (prepared as directed below)
¼ cup margarine or butter, softened
3 eggs
2 cups all purpose or unbleached flour
1½ teaspoons baking soda
1 teaspoon salt
¾ cup milk

Heat oven to 350°F. Grease and flour two 9-inch round cake pans. In large bowl, combine cream cheese, ½ cup margarine, vanilla and peppermint extract; blend until smooth. Add powdered sugar alternately with heated water; beat until smooth. Blend in chocolate.

In another large bowl, combine 2 cups of the frosting mixture and ¼ cup margarine; blend well. Beat in eggs, 1 at a time, beating well after each addition. Lightly spoon flour into measuring cup; level off. Add flour, baking soda, salt and milk; beat until smooth. Pour batter evenly into greased and floured pans. Bake at 350°F. for 30 to 40 minutes or until toothpick inserted in center comes out clean. Cool 5 minutes; remove from pans. Cool completely.

To assemble cake, place 1 layer, top side down, on serving plate; spread evenly with about ¼ of frosting. Top with remaining layer, top side up. Spread sides and top of cake with remaining frosting. **12 servings.**

HIGH ALTITUDE — Above 3500 Feet: Increase flour to 2½ cups. Use 1½ cups of the frosting mixture in cake. Bake as directed above.

NUTRIENTS PER 1/12 OF RECIPE
Calories	550	Sodium	380mg
Fat	23g	Potassium	110mg
Cholesterol	85mg		

DELICIOUS DEVIL'S FOOD CAKE

1½ cups all purpose or unbleached flour
1¼ cups sugar
½ cup unsweetened cocoa
1¼ teaspoons baking soda
1 teaspoon salt
1 cup buttermilk*
⅔ cup oil
1 teaspoon vanilla
2 eggs

Heat oven to 350°F. Grease and lightly flour bottoms only of two 8-inch round cake pans.** Lightly spoon flour into measuring cup; level off. In large bowl, combine flour and remaining ingredients at low speed until moistened; beat 3 minutes at medium speed. Pour batter into greased and floured pans. Bake at 350°F. for 25 to 30 minutes or until toothpick inserted in center comes out clean. Cool 5 minutes; remove from pans. Cool completely. Frost as desired. **12 servings.**

TIPS: *To substitute for buttermilk, use 1 tablespoon vinegar or lemon juice plus milk to make 1 cup.

**Cake can be baked in greased and lightly floured 13 × 9-inch pan. Bake 30 to 35 minutes.

HIGH ALTITUDE — Above 3500 Feet: Increase flour to 1½ cups plus 3 tablespoons. Bake at 375°F. for 25 to 30 minutes.

NUTRIENTS PER 1/12 OF RECIPE
Calories	280	Sodium	350mg
Fat	14g	Potassium	80mg
Cholesterol	47mg		

DOUBLE FUDGE FANCIFILL

FILLING
- ¼ cup sugar
- 1 tablespoon cornstarch
- 8-ounce package cream cheese, softened
- 2 tablespoons margarine or butter, softened
- 2 tablespoons milk
- ½ teaspoon vanilla
- 1 egg

CAKE
- 1 package pudding-included devil's food cake mix
- 1 cup water
- ⅓ cup oil
- 3 eggs

FROSTING
- 1 can ready-to-spread chocolate fudge frosting

Heat oven to 350°F. Grease and flour 13 × 9-inch pan. In small bowl, combine all filling ingredients; beat at highest speed until smooth. Set aside.

In large bowl, combine all cake ingredients at low speed until moistened; beat 2 minutes at highest speed. Pour half of batter into greased and floured pan. Pour filling mixture over batter; spread carefully to cover. Pour remaining batter evenly over filling.

Bake at 350°F. for 45 to 55 minutes or until toothpick inserted in center comes out clean. Cool completely. Spread frosting over top of cooled cake. Garnish as desired. Store in refrigerator. **16 servings.**

HIGH ALTITUDE — Above 3500 Feet: Omit milk in filling. Add ¼ cup flour to dry cake mix. Bake at 375°F. for 35 to 45 minutes.

NUTRIENTS PER 1/16 OF RECIPE

Calories	390	Sodium	410mg
Fat	21g	Potassium	140mg
Cholesterol	80mg		

CHOCOLATE MINT CREAM CAKE

CAKE
- 1 package pudding-included devil's food cake mix
- 1 cup water
- ½ cup oil
- ¼ cup creme de menthe liqueur or syrup
- 3 eggs

FROSTING
- 1½ cups whipping cream
- 3 tablespoons powdered sugar
- ¼ teaspoon mint extract
- **Candy Mint Trees (See Index)**

Heat oven to 350°F. Grease and flour two 8- or 9-inch round cake pans. In large bowl, combine all cake ingredients at low speed until moistened; beat 2 minutes at highest speed. Pour batter into greased and floured pans. Bake at 350°F. for 35 to 45 minutes or until toothpick inserted in center comes out clean. Cool 15 minutes; remove from pans. Cool completely.

In small bowl, beat whipping cream with powdered sugar and mint extract until stiff peaks form. To assemble cake, place 1 layer, bottom side up, on serving plate. Spread evenly with about ¼ of frosting. Top with remaining layer, top side up. Spread sides and top with remaining frosting. Garnish with Candy Mint Trees. Store in refrigerator. **12 servings.**

HIGH ALTITUDE — Above 3500 Feet: Increase water to 1 cup plus 4 teaspoons and add ¼ cup flour to dry cake mix. Bake at 375°F. for 30 to 40 minutes in greased and floured 9-inch round cake pans.

NUTRIENTS PER 1/12 OF RECIPE

Calories	410	Sodium	380mg
Fat	26g	Potassium	115mg
Cholesterol	110mg		

Double Fudge Fancifill

This recipe remains popular year after year. A cream cheese filling is baked between chocolaty layers, forming a creamy ribbon.

COOK'S NOTE
Whipping Cream

Before whipping cream, place the beaters and bowl in the refrigerator for 15 minutes to ensure firm, stiff peaks.

CHOCOLATE POUND CAKE

CAKE
3 cups sugar
1 cup margarine or butter, softened
½ cup shortening
1 teaspoon vanilla
5 eggs
3 cups all purpose or unbleached flour
¼ cup unsweetened cocoa
½ teaspoon baking powder
½ teaspoon salt
1 cup milk

GLAZE
2 tablespoons unsweetened cocoa
1 tablespoon water
1 tablespoon light corn syrup
2 tablespoons margarine or butter
¼ teaspoon vanilla
½ cup powdered sugar

Chocolate Pound Cake

———— ✎ ————

After greasing the pan for this taste-tempting chocolate cake, mix a little unsweetened cocoa with the flour used to dust the pan. This helps prevent a floury look on the baked cake.

Heat oven to 350°F. Grease and flour 10-inch tube pan. In large bowl, combine sugar, 1 cup margarine, shortening and 1 teaspooon vanilla; beat until light and fluffy. Add eggs 1 at a time, beating well after each addition. Lightly spoon flour into measuring cup; level off. In medium bowl, combine flour, ¼ cup cocoa, baking powder and salt. Alternately add flour mixture and milk to sugar mixture, beginning and ending with flour mixture and beating well after each addition. Pour batter into greased and floured pan. Bake at 350°F. for 70 to 85 minutes or until toothpick inserted in center comes out clean. Cool upright in pan 25 minutes; invert onto serving plate. Cool completely.

In small saucepan, combine 2 tablespoons cocoa, water, corn syrup and 2 tablespoons margarine. Cook over low heat until mixture thickens, stirring constantly. Remove from heat. Stir in ¼ teaspoon vanilla and powdered sugar; beat until smooth. Spread glaze over top of cooled cake, allowing some to run down sides. **16 servings.**

HIGH ALTITUDE — Above 3500 Feet: Increase flour to 3¼ cups. Bake at 375°F. for 70 to 80 minutes.

NUTRIENTS PER 1/16 OF RECIPE
Calories	460	Sodium	270mg
Fat	22g	Potassium	85mg
Cholesterol	90mg		

UPSIDE-DOWN GERMAN CHOCOLATE CAKE

FROSTING
¼ cup margarine or butter
¾ cup water
⅔ cup firmly packed brown sugar
1 cup coconut
1½ cups miniature marshmallows
½ cup chopped nuts

CAKE
1 package pudding-included German chocolate cake mix
1 cup water
½ cup dairy sour cream
⅓ cup oil
3 eggs

Upside-Down German Chocolate Cake

———— ✎ ————

The crunchy frosting for this deliciously rich cake is baked on the bottom. When serving the cake, use a large metal spatula to lift the pieces and invert onto serving plates.

Heat oven to 350°F. Grease and flour 13 × 9-inch pan. In small saucepan over low heat, melt ¼ cup margarine with ¾ cup water, stirring constantly. Stir in brown sugar. Spread evenly in greased and floured pan. Sprinkle coconut, marshmallows and nuts evenly over top.

In large bowl, combine all cake ingredients at low speed until moistened; beat 2 minutes at highest speed. Spoon batter evenly over topping mixture in pan. Bake at 350°F. for 38 to 48 minutes or until toothpick inserted in center comes out clean. Cool slightly. To serve, cut into squares; invert onto individual dessert plates. Serve warm or cool. **12 to 16 servings.**

HIGH ALTITUDE — Above 3500 Feet: Add 2 tablespoons flour to dry cake mix. Bake at 375°F. for 40 to 50 minutes.

NUTRIENTS PER 1/16 OF RECIPE
Calories	330	Sodium	300mg
Fat	17g	Potassium	125mg
Cholesterol	55mg		

Pictured top to bottom: Chocolate Pound Cake, page 50; Upside-Down German Chocolate Cake, page 50; Chocolate-Dipped Nuts, page 134

CHOCOLATE SOUR CREAM CAKE

Chocolate Sour Cream Cake

Cake fanciers who yearn for a touch of tradition will love this chocolate cake. To facilitate melting the chocolate, break the squares into smaller, uniform pieces.

Cookies 'n Cream Cake

Everyone loves chocolate sandwich cookies! In this recipe, they add pizzazz to a yummy white cake.

CAKE

2 cups all purpose or unbleached flour
2 cups sugar
1¼ teaspoons baking soda
1 teaspoon salt
½ teaspoon baking powder
1 cup water
¾ cup dairy sour cream
¼ cup shortening
1 teaspoon vanilla
2 eggs
4 ounces (4 squares) unsweetened chocolate, melted, cooled

FROSTING

3 cups powdered sugar
¼ cup dairy sour cream
¼ cup margarine or butter, softened
1 teaspoon vanilla
3 ounces (3 squares) unsweetened chocolate, melted, cooled

Heat oven to 350°F. Grease and flour two 8- or 9-inch round cake pans; line bottom of pans with waxed paper. Lightly spoon flour into measuring cup; level off. In medium bowl, combine flour, sugar, baking soda, salt and baking powder; blend well. In large bowl, combine remaining cake ingredients; add flour mixture. Blend at low speed until moistened; beat 3 minutes at highest speed. Pour batter into waxed paper-lined pans. Bake at 350°F. for 30 to 40 minutes or until toothpick inserted in center comes out clean. Cool 10 minutes; remove from pans. Cool completely.

In small bowl, combine all frosting ingredients; blend at low speed until moistened. Beat at highest speed until smooth and creamy.

To assemble cake, place 1 layer, top side down, on serving plate; spread evenly with about ¼ of frosting. Top with remaining layer, top side up. Spread sides and top of cake with remaining frosting. **12 servings.**

HIGH ALTITUDE—Above 3500 Feet: Decrease flour to 1½ cups and decrease water to ½ cup. Bake as directed above.

NUTRIENTS PER 1/12 OF RECIPE

Calories	580	Sodium	380mg
Fat	30g	Potassium	320mg
Cholesterol	55mg		

COOKIES 'N CREAM CAKE

CAKE

1 package pudding-included white cake mix
1¼ cups water
⅓ cup oil
3 egg whites
1 cup coarsely crushed creme-filled chocolate sandwich cookies

FROSTING

3 cups powdered sugar
¾ cup shortening
¼ cup milk
1 teaspoon vanilla

Heat oven to 350°F. Grease and flour 13 × 9-inch pan. In large bowl, combine all cake ingredients except crushed cookies at low speed until moistened; beat 2 minutes at highest speed. By hand, stir in cookies. Pour batter into greased and floured pan. Bake at 350°F. for 30 to 40 minutes or until toothpick inserted in center comes out clean. Cool completely.

In small bowl, combine all frosting ingredients; beat until smooth. Spread frosting over top of cooled cake. Garnish as desired. **12 servings.**

HIGH ALTITUDE—Above 3500 Feet: Add 3 tablespoons flour to dry cake mix. Increase water to 1⅓ cups. Bake at 375°F. for 20 to 30 minutes.

NUTRIENTS PER 1/12 OF RECIPE

Calories	500	Sodium	350mg
Fat	25g	Potassium	45mg
Cholesterol	2mg		

English Toffee Crunch Cake

ENGLISH TOFFEE CRUNCH CAKE

CAKE
    1 package pudding-included
      German chocolate cake mix
    1¼ cups water
    ⅓ cup oil
    3 eggs

FROSTING
    2 cups whipping cream
    ¼ teaspoon instant coffee granules
      or crystals
    3 tablespoons firmly packed
      brown sugar
    1 tablespoon chocolate-flavored
      liqueur, if desired
    6 (1⅛-ounce) English toffee candy
      bars

Heat oven to 350°F. Grease and flour two 8- or 9-inch round cake pans. In large bowl, combine all cake ingredients at low speed until moistened; beat 2 minutes at highest speed. Pour batter into greased and floured pans. Bake at 350°F. for 25 to 35 minutes or until toothpick inserted in center comes out clean. Cool 15 minutes; remove from pans. Cool completely.

In large bowl, beat whipping cream and instant coffee until slightly thickened. Add brown sugar; beat until stiff peaks form. Fold in liqueur. To assemble cake, slice each layer in half horizontally to make 4 layers. Place 1 layer on serving plate; spread with ½ cup of frosting. Crush 1 candy bar; sprinkle over frosting. Repeat with second and third layers. Spread remaining frosting over sides and top of cake. Coarsely chop remaining 3 candy bars; sprinkle on top and sides of cake. Refrigerate until ready to serve. Store in refrigerator. **12 servings.**

HIGH ALTITUDE—Above 3500 Feet: Add 2 tablespoons flour to dry cake mix. Bake at 375°F. for 25 to 35 minutes.

NUTRIENTS PER 1/12 OF RECIPE

Calories	520	Sodium	390mg
Fat	36g	Potassium	135mg
Cholesterol	120mg		

COOK'S NOTE
Preparing Cake Pans

Follow the directions for pan preparation stated in each recipe. Some cakes require that pans be greased on the bottom only. Others require greasing and flouring the entire pan. Always use solid shortening to grease pans.

"MY INSPIRATION" CAKE

CAKE
1 cup finely chopped pecans
1 package pudding-included white cake mix
1¼ cups water
⅓ cup oil
3 egg whites
2 ounces (2 squares) semi-sweet chocolate, grated

FROSTING
½ cup sugar
2 ounces (2 squares) unsweetened chocolate
¼ cup water
½ cup margarine or butter, softened
1 teaspoon vanilla
2¼ cups powdered sugar

Heat oven to 350°F. Grease and flour two 8- or 9-inch round cake pans. Sprinkle pecans evenly over bottom of each greased and floured pan. In a large bowl, combine cake mix, 1¼ cups water, oil and egg whites at low speed until moistened; beat 2 minutes at highest speed. Carefully spoon ¼ of batter into each nut-lined pan; sprinkle with grated chocolate. Spoon remaining batter over grated chocolate; spread carefully. Bake at 350°F. for 20 to 28 minutes or until toothpick inserted in center comes out clean. Cool 15 minutes; remove from pans. Cool completely.

To make frosting, in small saucepan over low heat, melt sugar and unsweetened chocolate in ¼ cup water, stirring constantly until smooth. Remove from heat; cool. In small bowl, beat margarine and vanilla until smooth. Gradually blend in powdered sugar. Reserve ⅓ cup of margarine mixture. Add cooled chocolate mixture to remaining margarine mixture; beat until smooth.

To assemble cake, place 1 layer, nut side up, on serving plate; spread with ⅓ (about ½ cup) of chocolate frosting. Top with remaining layer, nut side up. Frost sides and ½ inch around top edge

of cake with remaining chocolate frosting. Spoon or pipe reserved white frosting around edge of nuts on top of cake.*12 servings.

TIP: *If necessary, add water, 1 drop at a time, to white frosting for desired piping consistency.

HIGH ALTITUDE — Above 3500 Feet: Add 3 tablespoons flour to dry cake mix and increase water to 1⅓ cups.

NUTRIENTS PER 1/12 OF RECIPE

Calories	530	Sodium	390mg
Fat	29g	Potassium	170mg
Cholesterol	0mg		

SAUCEPAN CHOCOLATE CAKE

2 cups all purpose or unbleached flour
2 cups sugar
1 teaspoon baking soda
1 cup margarine or butter
1 cup water
¼ cup unsweetened cocoa
½ cup buttermilk*
1 teaspoon vanilla
2 eggs

Heat oven to 375°F. Grease and flour 13×9-inch pan. Lightly spoon flour into measuring cup; level off. In medium bowl, combine flour, sugar and baking soda; set aside. In large saucepan, combine margarine, water and cocoa; bring to a boil. Remove from heat. Add flour mixture, buttermilk, vanilla and eggs. By hand, beat about 2 minutes. Pour batter into greased and floured pan. Bake at 375°F. for 20 to 30 minutes or until toothpick inserted in center comes out clean. Cool completely. Frost as desired. **12 servings.**

TIP: *To substitute for buttermilk, use 1½ teaspoons vinegar or lemon juice plus milk to make ½ cup.

HIGH ALTITUDE — Above 3500 Feet: No change.

NUTRIENTS PER 1/12 OF RECIPE

Calories	360	Sodium	310mg
Fat	17g	Potassium	65mg
Cholesterol	46mg		

"My Inspiration" Cake

This cake won the Grand Prize in the 1953 Bake-Off® Contest. Each layer has a chocolate surprise and a toasted nut topping baked right in.

COOK'S NOTE
Pans for Baking Cakes

For even browning and a tender cake texture, choose shiny metal pans or those with a nonstick finish.

There is a direct correlation between pan size or style and the amount or type of batter. Just as substituting ingredients can cause problems, so can substituting pan types and sizes. The recipes in this book have been developed and tested with the pans indicated in each recipe.

CHOCOLATE PRALINE LAYER CAKE

CAKE
- ½ cup butter or margarine
- ¼ cup whipping cream
- 1 cup firmly packed brown sugar
- ¾ cup coarsely chopped pecans
- 1 package pudding-included devil's food cake mix
- 1¼ cups water
- ⅓ cup oil
- 3 eggs

TOPPING
- 1¾ cups whipping cream
- ¼ cup powdered sugar
- ¼ teaspoon vanilla
  Whole pecans, if desired
  Chocolate Curls, if desired (See Index)

Heat oven to 325°F. In small heavy saucepan, combine butter, ¼ cup whipping cream and brown sugar. Cook over low heat just until butter is melted, stirring occasionally. Pour evenly into two 9- or 8-inch round cake pans; sprinkle each evenly with chopped pecans. In large bowl, combine cake mix, water, oil and eggs at low speed until moistened; beat 2 minutes at highest speed. Carefully spoon ¼ of batter over pecan mixture around edge of one pan; fill center of pan with ¼ of batter. Repeat with remaining batter and pan. Bake at 325°F. for 35 to 45 minutes or until top springs back when touched lightly in center. Cool 5 minutes; remove from pans. Cool completely.

In small bowl, beat 1¾ cups whipping cream, powdered sugar, and vanilla until stiff peaks form.

To assemble cake, place 1 layer, praline side up, on serving plate. Spread top with ½ of topping. Top with remaining layer, praline side up. Spread top with remaining topping. Garnish with whole pecans and chocolate curls. Store in refrigerator. **12 servings.**

HIGH ALTITUDE — Above 3500 Feet: Add 2 tablespoons flour to dry cake mix. Increase water to 1⅓ cups. Bake at 350°F. for 30 to 35 minutes. Immediately remove from pans.

NUTRIENTS PER 1/12 OF RECIPE

Calories	610	Sodium	470mg
Fat	41g	Potassium	230mg
Cholesterol	140mg		

HOT FUDGE PUDDING CAKE

- 1¼ cups all purpose or unbleached flour
- ¾ cup sugar
- 2 tablespoons unsweetened cocoa
- 1½ teaspoons baking powder
- ½ teaspoon salt
- ½ cup milk
- 2 tablespoons margarine or butter, melted
- 1 teaspoon vanilla
- 1 cup sugar
- 2 tablespoons unsweetened cocoa
  Dash salt
- 1⅓ cups water heated to 115 to 120°F.
  Whipped cream or favorite flavor ice cream, if desired

Heat oven to 350°F. Lightly spoon flour into measuring cup; level off. In small bowl, combine flour, ¾ cup sugar, 2 tablespoons cocoa, baking powder and ½ teaspoon salt. Stir in milk, margarine and vanilla; blend well. Spread batter in ungreased 9-inch round or square pan.

In small bowl, combine 1 cup sugar, 2 tablespoons cocoa and dash salt; sprinkle evenly over cake batter. Pour water over sugar-cocoa mixture. Bake at 350°F. for 35 to 45 minutes or until center is set and firm to the touch. Serve warm. Top with whipped cream or ice cream. **8 servings.**

HIGH ALTITUDE — Above 3500 Feet: No change.

NUTRIENTS PER 1/8 OF RECIPE

Calories	340	Sodium	320mg
Fat	9g	Potassium	75mg
Cholesterol	20mg		

Hot Fudge Pudding Cake

The whole family will love this old-fashioned dessert. It makes its own fudge sauce as it bakes.

COOK'S NOTE
Greasing and Flouring Pans

This is a convenient method for greasing and flouring pans. In small bowl, blend 1 cup shortening and 1 cup all purpose flour until well mixed. Store in airtight container. To grease and flour pan, use pastry brush dipped in shortening-flour mixture.

Triple Chocolate Cake; White Chocolate Piping, page 128

TRIPLE CHOCOLATE CAKE

CAKE

    1 package pudding-included
      devil's food cake mix
    1 cup dairy sour cream
    ¾ cup water
    ⅓ cup oil
    3 eggs
    4-ounce bar milk chocolate,
      chopped

FROSTING

    8-ounce white baking bar, cut into
      pieces
    ¾ cup butter or margarine,
      softened
    ½ cup powdered sugar

Heat oven to 350°F. Grease and flour
two 9-inch round cake pans. In large
bowl, combine cake mix, sour cream,
water, oil and eggs at low speed until
moistened; beat 2 minutes at highest
speed. Gently fold in milk chocolate.

Pour batter evenly into greased and
floured pans. Bake at 350°F. for 30 to
40 minutes or until top springs back
when touched lightly in center. Cool
15 minutes; remove from pans. Cool
completely.

In small saucepan over low heat, melt
white baking bar, stirring constantly
until smooth. Remove from heat; cool.
In small bowl, combine butter and
powdered sugar; beat until fluffy.
Gradually beat in cooled baking bar
until smooth and fluffy. To assemble
cake, place 1 layer, bottom side up, on
serving plate; spread ½ cup frosting
over layer. Place remaining layer, bottom side down, on frosted layer. Spread
remaining frosting over sides and top
of cake. Garnish as desired. **16 servings.**

HIGH ALTITUDE—Above 3500
Feet: Add ¼ cup flour to dry cake mix.
Bake as directed above.

NUTRIENTS PER 1/16 OF RECIPE

Calories	430	Sodium	370mg
Fat	27g	Potassium	230mg
Cholesterol	90mg		

TUNNEL OF FUDGE™ CAKE

CAKE
1¾ cups sugar

1¾ cups margarine or butter, softened

6 eggs

2 cups powdered sugar

2¼ cups all purpose or unbleached flour

¾ cup unsweetened cocoa

2 cups chopped walnuts*

GLAZE
¾ cup powdered sugar

¼ cup unsweetened cocoa

1½ to 2 tablespoons milk

Heat oven to 350°F. Grease and flour 12-cup fluted tube pan or 10-inch tube pan. In large bowl, combine sugar and margarine; beat until light and fluffy. Add eggs 1 at a time, beating well after each addition. Gradually add 2 cups powdered sugar; blend well. Lightly spoon flour into measuring cup; level off. By hand, stir in flour and remaining cake ingredients until well blended. Spoon batter into greased and floured pan; spread evenly. Bake at 350°F. for 58 to 62 minutes.** Cool upright in pan on wire rack 1 hour; invert onto serving plate. Cool completely.

In small bowl, blend ¾ cup powdered sugar, ¼ cup cocoa and enough milk for desired drizzling consistency. Spoon over top of cake, allowing some to run down sides. Store tightly covered.

16 servings.

TIPS: *Nuts are essential for the success of this recipe.

**Since this cake has a soft tunnel of fudge, an ordinary doneness test cannot be used. Accurate oven temperature and baking time are essential.

HIGH ALTITUDE—Above 3500 Feet: Increase flour to 2¼ cups plus 3 tablespoons. Bake as directed above.

NUTRIENTS PER 1/16 OF RECIPE

Calories	550	Sodium	300mg
Fat	33g	Potassium	170mg
Cholesterol	100mg		

CHOCOLATE BANANA SNACK CAKE

1 cup rolled oats

½ cup margarine or butter

1¼ cups boiling water

¾ cup honey

1 teaspoon vanilla

¾ cup (2 medium) mashed bananas

2 eggs

1¾ cups whole wheat flour

1½ teaspoons baking soda

1 teaspoon cinnamon

½ teaspoon salt

¼ teaspoon nutmeg

½ cup flaked coconut

½ cup chopped walnuts

1 cup semi-sweet chocolate chips

Heat oven to 350°F. Grease and flour 13×9-inch pan. In large bowl, combine rolled oats, margarine and water; let stand 20 minutes. Stir in honey, vanilla, bananas and eggs; blend well. Lightly spoon flour into measuring cup; level off. In small bowl, combine flour, baking soda, cinnamon, salt and nutmeg. By hand, stir into oat-banana mixture until well blended. Fold in coconut, walnuts and chocolate chips. Pour batter into greased and floured pan. Bake at 350°F. for 35 to 40 minutes or until top springs back when touched lightly in center. (Cake will not rise high.) Serve warm or cool.

15 servings.

HIGH ALTITUDE—Above 3500 Feet: Decrease baking soda to 1¼ teaspoons. Bake as directed above.

NUTRIENTS PER 1/15 OF RECIPE

Calories	310	Sodium	320mg
Fat	15g	Potassium	220mg
Cholesterol	35mg		

Tunnel of Fudge™ Cake

This rich moist cake is the un-disputed favorite of all Pillsbury chocolate recipes. When this recipe won a prize in the 1966 Bake-Off® Contest, it was made with a frosting mix that is no longer available. Because of its great popularity, the recipe has been revised to make the fudgy tunnel from scratch.

Chocolate Banana Snack Cake

It's easy to stir this whole wheat banana cake together by hand. Serve it warm for a great snack or dessert.

PEANUT BUTTER CUPS

DOUBLE CHOCOLATE CHUNK CUPCAKES

Double Chocolate Chunk Cupcakes

The cocoa-flavored dough for these cupcakes is full of white and milk chocolate chips. The cupcakes are so good themselves that there's no need for frosting.

1¾ cups all purpose or unbleached flour
1¼ cups firmly packed brown sugar
3 teaspoons baking powder
1 teaspoon salt
1 cup milk
⅓ cup shortening
⅓ cup peanut butter
1 teaspoon vanilla
2 eggs
24 miniature milk chocolate-covered peanut butter cups, unwrapped

Heat oven to 350°F. Line 24 muffin cups with paper baking cups. Lightly spoon flour into measuring cup; level off. In large bowl, combine all ingredients except peanut butter cups; blend at low speed until moistened. Beat 2 minutes at medium speed. Fill paper-lined muffin cups ⅔ full. Press 1 peanut butter cup into batter in each muffin cup until top edge of candy is even with top of batter. Bake at 350°F. for 18 to 28 minutes or until tops spring back when touched lightly in center. Serve warm or cool. **24 cupcakes.**

HIGH ALTITUDE—Above 3500 Feet: No change.

NUTRIENTS PER 1 CUPCAKE

Calories	170	Sodium	180mg
Fat	7g	Potassium	125mg
Cholesterol	25mg		

2 cups all purpose or unbleached flour
½ cup firmly packed brown sugar
¼ cup unsweetened cocoa
1 teaspoon baking soda
¼ teaspoon salt
1 cup buttermilk*
½ cup margarine or butter, melted
½ teaspoon almond extract
1 egg
½ cup vanilla milk chips or 3 ounces white baking bar, chopped
½ cup milk chocolate chips
¼ cup chopped slivered almonds

Heat oven to 375°F. Grease 18 muffin cups. Lightly spoon flour into measuring cup; level off. In large bowl, combine flour, brown sugar, cocoa, baking soda and salt; blend well. Add buttermilk, margarine, almond extract and egg; blend just until dry ingredients are moistened. Fold in chips and almonds. Fill greased muffin cups ¾ full. Bake at 375°F. for 15 to 20 minutes or until toothpick inserted in center comes out clean. Cool 3 minutes; remove from muffin cups. Serve warm or cool. **18 cupcakes.**

TIP: *To substitute for buttermilk, use 1 tablespoon vinegar or lemon juice plus milk to make 1 cup.

HIGH ALTITUDE—Above 3500 Feet: No change.

NUTRIENTS PER 1 CUPCAKE

Calories	200	Sodium	190mg
Fat	10g	Potassium	120mg
Cholesterol	15mg		

Chocolate Lover's Cake; Chocolate Curls, page 128

CHOCOLATE LOVER'S CAKE

CAKE
1 package pudding-included
    devil's food cake mix
1 cup dairy sour cream
¾ cup water
⅓ cup oil
3 eggs
4-ounce bar milk chocolate,
    grated

FILLING
1 cup whipping cream, whipped,
    sweetened
21-ounce can cherry fruit pie filling
¼ cup sliced almonds
    Chocolate Curls, if desired (See
    Index)

Heat oven to 350°F. Grease and flour two 9-inch round cake pans. In large bowl, combine all cake ingredients except grated chocolate at low speed until moistened; beat 2 minutes at highest speed. Gently fold in grated chocolate. Pour batter evenly into greased and floured pans. Bake at 350°F. for 35 to 45 minutes or until top springs back when touched lightly in center. Cool 15 minutes; remove from pans. Cool completely.

To assemble cake, place 1 layer, bottom side up, on serving plate. Spoon or pipe 1 cup of the whipped cream around top edge of layer. Spoon half of the cherry pie filling over center of layer. Top with remaining layer, top side up. Spoon remaining cherry pie filling in heart shape onto center of cake. Spoon or pipe remaining whipped cream around edge of heart. Garnish with almonds and Chocolate Curls. Store in refrigerator. **16 servings.**

HIGH ALTITUDE — Above 3500 Feet: Add ¼ cup flour to dry cake mix. Increase water to 1⅓ cups. Bake at 375°F. for 30 to 40 minutes.

NUTRIENTS PER 1/16 OF RECIPE

Calories	400	Sodium	270mg
Fat	21g	Potassium	240mg
Cholesterol	80mg		

Chocolate Lover's Cake

Famous German dessert flavors, chocolate and cherry, combine in this moist, chocolaty cake. Enjoy the goodness of Old World baking with updated convenience.

GANACHE LAYERED CREAM TORTE

Ganache Layered Cream Torte

A ganache is basically a mixture of whipping cream, chocolate and margarine that is melted, cooled and whipped. Besides being light and luscious, this filling is new, trendy and so simple.

Chocolate Strawberry Shortcake

This is an impressive recipe that tastes wonderful. For the best-quality strawberries, choose firm, bright red berries with no soft or bruised spots.

CAKE
1 package pudding-included
   devil's food cake mix
1 cup dairy sour cream
¾ cup water
⅓ cup oil
3 eggs
1 cup miniature semi-sweet
   chocolate chips

FILLING
1½ cups whipping cream
8 ounces (8 squares) semi-sweet
   chocolate, chopped
¼ cup margarine or butter
   Chocolate Curls (See Index)
   Powdered sugar

Heat oven to 350°F. Grease and flour two 9-inch round cake pans. In large bowl, combine cake mix, sour cream, water, oil and eggs at low speed until moistened; beat 2 minutes at highest speed. By hand, stir in chocolate chips. Pour batter into greased and floured pans. Bake at 350°F. for 35 to 45 minutes or until toothpick inserted in center comes out clean. Cool 15 minutes; remove from pans. Cool completely.

In medium saucepan over medium heat, combine whipping cream, chocolate and margarine, stirring constantly until mixture is smooth and begins to boil. Remove from heat. Refrigerate for at least 1 hour or until well chilled. With hand mixer, beat chocolate mixture until light and fluffy.

To assemble torte, slice each cake layer in half horizontally to make 4 layers. Place 1 layer on serving plate; spread with ¼ of filling mixture. Repeat with second and third layers. Top with remaining layer; spread remaining filling over top of torte. Refrigerate until ready to serve. Garnish with Chocolate Curls and powdered sugar. Let stand at room temperature about 10 minutes

before serving. Store in refrigerator
16 servings.

HIGH ALTITUDE — Above 3500 Feet: Add 3 tablespoons flour to dry cake mix. Bake at 375°F. for 40 to 45 minutes.

NUTRIENTS PER 1/16 OF RECIPE
Calories	510	Sodium	330mg
Fat	35g	Potassium	210mg
Cholesterol	90mg		

CHOCOLATE STRAWBERRY SHORTCAKE

SHORTCAKE
2 cups all purpose or unbleached
   flour
½ cup sugar
⅓ cup unsweetened cocoa
3 teaspoons baking powder
¼ teaspoon salt
½ cup butter or margarine
1 cup milk
2 tablespoons sugar

FILLING
4 to 5 cups fresh strawberries
¼ cup sugar
2 cups whipping cream, whipped,
   sweetened
   Fudge sauce, if desired

Heat oven to 400°F. Grease two 9- or 8-inch round cake pans. Lightly spoon flour into measuring cup; level off. In large bowl, combine flour, ½ cup sugar, cocoa, baking powder and salt. With pastry blender or fork, cut in butter until mixture resembles coarse crumbs. With a fork, stir in milk until just moistened. Spread dough in greased pans. Sprinkle 2 tablespoons sugar over dough. Bake at 400°F. for 15 to 20 minutes or until shortcake begins to pull away from sides of pans. Cool 15 minutes; remove from pans. Cool completely.

Chocolate Strawberry Shortcake

Reserve 5 whole strawberries for garnish. Hull and halve remaining strawberries. In large bowl, combine halved strawberries and ¼ cup sugar. To assemble shortcake, place 1 layer, bottom side up, on serving plate. Top with half of the strawberries and half of the whipped cream. Top with remaining layer, top side up. Top with remaining strawberries and whipped cream. Garnish with reserved whole strawberries. Drizzle with fudge sauce. **12 servings.**

HIGH ALTITUDE – Above 3500 Feet: No change.

NUTRIENTS PER 1/12 OF RECIPE (without fudge sauce)

Calories	440	Sodium	260mg
Fat	24g	Potassium	280mg
Cholesterol	77mg		

DARK CHOCOLATE SACHER TORTE

CAKE
½ cup finely chopped dried
   apricots
½ cup rum*
1 package pudding-included dark
   chocolate cake mix
¾ cup water
⅓ cup oil
3 eggs

GLAZE
2 (10-ounce) jars apricot
   preserves
2 tablespoons rum**

FROSTING
6-ounce package (1 cup) semi-
   sweet chocolate chips
¾ cup margarine or butter
½ to 1 cup sliced almonds

Heat oven to 350°F. Grease and flour two 9- or 8-inch round cake pans. In small bowl, combine apricots and ½ cup rum; let stand 10 minutes. In large bowl, combine apricot-rum mixture and remaining cake ingredients at low speed until moistened; beat 2 minutes at highest speed. Pour into greased and floured pans. Bake at 350°F. Bake 9-inch layers 25 to 35 minutes, 8-inch layers 35 to 45 minutes or until toothpick inserted in center comes out clean. Cool 15 minutes; remove from pans. Cool completely.

In small saucepan over low heat, melt glaze ingredients; strain to remove large apricot pieces. To assemble torte, carefully slice each layer in half horizontally to make 4 layers. Place 1 layer on serving plate; spread with ¼ cup glaze. Repeat with remaining layers and glaze, ending with cake layer. Spread remaining ¼ cup glaze over top of torte, allowing some to run down sides. Refrigerate 1 hour or until glaze is set.

In small saucepan over low heat, melt chocolate chips and butter, stirring constantly until smooth. Refrigerate 30 minutes or until slightly thickened, stirring occasionally. Spread frosting over sides and top of cake. Arrange 6 almond slices on top of cake. Press remaining almond slices into frosting on sides of cake. Refrigerate at least 1 hour before serving. Garnish as desired. Store in refrigerator. **16 servings.**

TIPS: *To substitute for ½ cup rum in cake, use 2 teaspoons rum extract plus water to make ½ cup.

**To substitute for 2 tablespoons rum in glaze, use 1 teaspoon rum extract plus water to make 2 tablespoons.

HIGH ALTITUDE—Above 3500 Feet: Add 3 tablespoons flour to dry cake mix. Bake at 375°F. for 30 to 40 minutes.

NUTRIENTS PER 1/16 OF RECIPE

Calories	470	Sodium	390mg
Fat	25g	Potassium	220mg
Cholesterol	51mg		

Dark Chocolate Sacher Torte

This wonderful torte is inspired by the European dessert. For a most impressive presentation, garnish it with an apricot rose and Chocolate Leaves (See Index).

COOK'S NOTE
Apricot Rose

To create an apricot rose, sprinkle sugar on waxed paper. Place dried apricot halves on sugar. Sprinkle with additional sugar. Place a second sheet of waxed paper over the apricot halves and press until double in size. Roll up one half tightly to form center of rose. Loosely wrap the remaining halves around the center, overlapping slightly and shaping the edges like rose petals. Press together at the base and trim if necessary. Place the apricot rose on the frosted cake.

CHOCOLATE SILK BUTTERCREAM FROSTING

2 ounces (2 squares) semi-sweet chocolate, cut into pieces
1 ounce (1 square) unsweetened chocolate, cut into pieces
⅓ cup sugar
¼ cup water
1 cup powdered sugar
1 cup unsalted butter, salted butter or margarine, cut into small pieces, softened

In small saucepan over low heat, melt semi-sweet and unsweetened chocolate, stirring constantly until smooth. Remove from heat. In another small saucepan, bring sugar and water to a boil; boil 1 minute. Remove from heat.

Place powdered sugar in medium bowl. Gradually add sugar-water mixture; beat at highest speed 5 minutes or until smooth. Gradually add butter 1 small piece at a time, beating well after each addition. Add melted chocolate; beat until smooth. Frost cooled cake or bars. **2 cups** (frosts 2-layer or 13 × 9-inch cake).

NUTRIENTS PER 1/12 OF RECIPE

Calories	230	Sodium	0mg
Fat	18g	Potassium	40mg
Cholesterol	41mg		

COCOA-LITE FROSTING

⅓ cup margarine or butter, softened
2 cups powdered sugar
1 tablespoon unsweetened cocoa
½ teaspoon vanilla
1 to 2 tablespoons milk

In small bowl, beat margarine until fluffy. Add powdered sugar, cocoa, vanilla and enough milk for desired spreading consistency. Frost cooled cake. **About 1 cup** (frosts 8- or 9-inch square cake).

NUTRIENTS PER 1/9 OF RECIPE

Calories	150	Sodium	85mg
Fat	7g	Potassium	15mg
Cholesterol	0mg		

WHITE BUTTERCREAM FROSTING

6 ounces vanilla-flavored candy coating, cut into pieces
3 to 4 tablespoons chocolate-flavored liqueur
¾ cup butter, softened
¼ cup powdered sugar

In small saucepan over low heat, melt candy coating, stirring constantly until smooth. Remove from heat; stir in chocolate liqueur. Cool 30 minutes.

In small bowl, combine butter and powdered sugar; beat until light and fluffy. Gradually beat in cooled candy coating mixture until smooth. Frost cooled cake or bars. **About 2 cups** (frosts 2-layer or 13 × 9-inch cake).

NUTRIENTS PER 1/12 OF RECIPE

Calories	210	Sodium	130mg
Fat	18g	Potassium	90mg
Cholesterol	34mg		

CREAM CHEESE CHOCOLATE FROSTING

3-ounce package cream cheese, softened
2 cups powdered sugar
6-ounce package (1 cup) semi-sweet chocolate chips, melted, cooled
3 tablespoons milk
1 teaspoon vanilla

In small bowl, combine cream cheese and powdered sugar; beat at medium speed until light and fluffy. Blend in melted chocolate, milk and vanilla at low speed until smooth. If necessary, add additional milk 1 teaspoon at a time for desired spreading consistency. Frost cooled cake or bars. Store in refrigerator. **1¾ cups** (frosts 2-layer or 13 × 9-inch cake).

NUTRIENTS PER 1/12 OF RECIPE

Calories	160	Sodium	25mg
Fat	8g	Potassium	60mg
Cholesterol	8mg		

Chocolate Silk Pecan Pie, page 70

Pies, Tarts & Meringues

In merrie olde England, "pye" almost always meant a meat mixture baked in a small casserole with a pastry crust on top. If it were not for the American invention of dessert pies, we would miss out on the luscious chocolate pies and tarts featured here.

Most tarts are baked in a fluted pan, often with a removable bottom so the tart can be taken from the pan and presented whole at the table on a fancy plate. Tart preparation is simple, calling for basic pastry techniques and utensils.

To streamline pie and tart preparation, many of these recipes feature refrigerated pie crust, which is simply unfolded and shaped in the pan for baking. It's as light, flaky and delicious as the best homemade pie crust. You'll also find easy-to-make crusts of coconut and chocolate cookie crumbs and meringue.

Meringues take some time to prepare, but preparation is not difficult. At serving time, simply top baked-ahead meringue with a fancy filling to create an eye-catching dessert like Chocolate Toffee Cloud.

You don't need to be one bit hungry to crave the chocolate delicacies featured here—mounds of chocolate mousse in a meringue shell, creamy fudge in a macaroon crust and a chocolate, caramel and almond concoction to rival the most exquisite candy bar.

Many of the recipes team chocolate with fruit for truly ambrosial tastes. Linzer Tart features a chocolate cookie crust that's flavored with hazelnuts and topped with raspberry jam and whipped cream for a dessert that's nothing short of sensational. And Banana Split Pie combines the requisites of the original dessert, including strawberry ice cream, fudge and pineapple toppings, pecans and bananas—all in a prepared chocolate crumb crust.

Our most requested pie, Creamy French Silk, is included in here, but we think that every recipe in this collection will earn "most requested" status in your home.

TIMESAVING GERMAN CHOCOLATE PIE

CRUST
15-ounce package refrigerated pie crusts
1 teaspoon flour

FILLING
4-ounce bar sweet cooking chocolate, chopped
¼ cup margarine or butter
1 teaspoon vanilla
3 eggs
1 can ready-to-spread coconut pecan frosting
3 tablespoons flour
Whipped cream, if desired

Prepare pie crust according to package directions for *filled one-crust pie* using 9-inch pie pan. (Refrigerate remaining crust for later use.) Heat oven to 350°F.

In small saucepan over low heat, melt chocolate and margarine, stirring constantly until smooth. Remove from heat; stir in vanilla. In small bowl, beat eggs until well blended. Add frosting and 3 tablespoons flour; blend well. Stir in chocolate mixture. Pour into pie crust-lined pan. Bake at 350°F. for 45 to 55 minutes or until knife inserted near edge comes out clean. (Filling puffs up during baking.) Cool completely. Serve with whipped cream. Store in refrigerator. **10 servings.**

NUTRIENTS PER 1/10 OF RECIPE

Calories	420	Sodium	280mg
Fat	28g	Potassium	130mg
Cholesterol	80mg		

BAVARIAN CHOCOLATE RIPPLE CREAM PIE

CRUST
1 cup finely crushed crisp coconut macaroon cookies
½ cup finely chopped almonds
⅓ cup firmly packed brown sugar
¼ cup all purpose or unbleached flour
⅓ cup margarine or butter, melted

FILLING
1 envelope unflavored gelatin
1¾ cups milk
¾ cup sugar
2 ounces (2 squares) semi-sweet chocolate, chopped
2 tablespoons margarine or butter
1 teaspoon vanilla
1 cup whipping cream, whipped
Grated Chocolate (See Index)

Heat oven to 350°F. In small bowl, combine all crust ingredients. Press in bottom and up sides of 9-inch pie pan. Bake at 350°F. for 15 minutes. Cool.

In small saucepan, soften gelatin in 1 cup of the milk; let stand 5 minutes. Add sugar and chocolate. Cook over medium heat, stirring constantly until mixture just begins to boil and chocolate is melted. Remove from heat; stir in 2 tablespoons margarine until smooth. Add remaining ¾ cup milk and vanilla; blend well. Refrigerate until almost set.

Spread ¼ of chocolate mixture in cooled baked crust. Spread ¼ of whipped cream over chocolate. Repeat layers with remaining chocolate mixture and whipped cream, ending with whipped cream. To marble, pull knife through top 2 layers in wide curves. Refrigerate at least 2 hours before serving. Garnish with Grated Chocolate. Store in refrigerator. **8 servings.**

NUTRIENTS PER 1/8 OF RECIPE

Calories	500	Sodium	170mg
Fat	32g	Potassium	290mg
Cholesterol	60mg		

Bavarian Chocolate Ripple Cream Pie

Our taste panel was crazy about this pie! It has a tasty macaroon crust and rippled layers of chocolate and whipped cream — mmm.

COOK'S NOTE
Storing Pies Containing Dairy Products

All pies containing dairy products (milk, sour cream, whipped cream or topping, ice cream, yogurt, cream cheese, etc.) should be refrigerated or frozen as soon as possible following preparation, particularly in warm weather. This will prevent spoilage and deterioration in flavor and texture.

Bavarian Chocolate Ripple Cream Pie, page 66; Grated Chocolate, page 131

Black Forest Tart; Chocolate Filigree Hearts, page 128

BLACK FOREST TART

CRUST
   15-ounce package refrigerated pie crusts
   1 teaspoon flour

FILLING
   6 ounces (6 squares) semi-sweet chocolate, cut into pieces
   2 tablespoons margarine or butter
   ¼ cup powdered sugar
   8-ounce package cream cheese, softened
   21-ounce can cherry fruit pie filling

TOPPING
   1 cup whipping cream
   1 ounce (1 square) semi-sweet chocolate, grated
   Chocolate Curls, if desired (See Index)

Heat oven to 450°F. Prepare pie crust according to package directions for *unfilled one-crust pie* using 9-inch pie pan or 10-inch tart pan with removable bottom. (Refrigerate remaining crust for later use.) Bake at 450°F. for 9 to 11 minutes or until golden brown. Cool.

In small saucepan over low heat, melt 6 ounces chocolate and margarine, stirring constantly until smooth. In small bowl, combine powdered sugar and cream cheese; blend until smooth. Stir in chocolate mixture; beat until smooth. Add 1 cup of the cherry filling; stir gently. Set aside remaining cherry filling. Spread mixture evenly in cooled baked crust. Refrigerate 1 hour.

In small bowl, beat whipped cream until stiff peaks form. Gently fold in grated chocolate. Spread evenly over chilled chocolate layer. Spoon remaining pie filling in a ring around outer edge of tart. Refrigerate until serving time. Garnish with Chocolate Curls. Store in refrigerator. **12 servings.**

NUTRIENTS PER 1/12 OF RECIPE

Calories	430	Sodium	160mg
Fat	27g	Potassium	140mg
Cholesterol	50mg		

Black Forest Tart

This elegant tart can be made well in advance of serving, since it refrigerates well. Garnish each piece with chocolate curls.

RASPBERRY FUDGE RIBBON PIE

15-ounce package refrigerated pie crusts
1 teaspoon flour
4 ounces (4 squares) semi-sweet chocolate, cut into pieces
¼ cup whipping cream

FILLING
3 cups fresh raspberries
1 cup sugar
3 tablespoons cornstarch
1 cup cold water
2 tablespoons corn syrup
2 tablespoons raspberry-flavored gelatin

Whipped cream, if desired

MICROWAVE DIRECTIONS:

Prepare pie crust according to package microwave directions for *unfilled one-crust pie* using 9-inch microwave-safe pie pan. (Refrigerate remaining crust for later use.)

In 2-cup microwave-safe measuring cup, combine chocolate and whipping cream. Microwave on MEDIUM for 1½ to 2 minutes or until chocolate is melted, stirring once halfway through cooking. Stir until smooth. Spread chocolate mixture in bottom of cooked crust. Cool. Refrigerate until chocolate is firm.

Arrange raspberries over top of chocolate layer. In 4-cup microwave-safe measuring cup, combine sugar and cornstarch; blend well. Stir in water and corn syrup. Microwave on HIGH for 4 to 4½ minutes or until mixture boils, stirring once halfway through cooking. Boil 1 minute. Stir in gelatin until dissolved; pour over berries. Refrigerate until set. Just before serving, spoon or pipe whipped cream around edge of pie. **10 servings.**

NUTRIENTS PER 1/10 OF RECIPE

Calories	310	Sodium	135mg
Fat	13g	Potassium	110mg
Cholesterol	15mg		

CHOCOLATE MOUSSE ANGEL PIE

MERINGUE SHELL
3 egg whites, room temperature
¼ teaspoon cream of tartar
Dash salt
¾ cup sugar
½ teaspoon vanilla

FILLING
6-ounce package (1 cup) semi-sweet chocolate chips
¼ cup water
⅛ to ¼ teaspoon almond extract
1½ cups whipping cream, whipped
Toasted sliced almonds*

Heat oven to 275°F. Generously butter 9-inch pie pan. In small bowl, combine egg whites, cream of tartar and salt; beat until foamy. Gradually add sugar; beat until stiff peaks form. Add vanilla; blend well. Using a metal spatula, spread egg white mixture over bottom and sides of buttered pan, building up sides as high as possible. Bake at 275°F. for 1 hour. Turn oven off. Let stand in oven with door ajar for 1 hour. Remove meringue shell from oven. Cool completely.

In small saucepan over low heat, melt chocolate chips with water, stirring constantly until smooth. Remove from heat; stir in almond extract. Cool. Place 2 cups of the whipped cream in a small bowl. Gently fold chocolate mixture into whipped cream. Spread filling in cooled baked meringue shell. Garnish with remaining whipped cream and sliced almonds. Store in refrigerator. **8 servings.**

TIP: *To toast almonds, spread on cookie sheet; bake at 375°F. for 5 to 10 minutes or until light golden brown, stirring occasionally. Or spread thin layer in microwave-safe pie pan. Microwave on HIGH for 3 to 4 minutes or until light golden brown, stirring frequently.

NUTRIENTS PER 1/8 OF RECIPE

Calories	380	Sodium	55mg
Fat	26g	Potassium	140mg
Cholesterol	60mg		

Raspberry Fudge Ribbon Pie

Luscious glazed raspberries over rich chocolate make this flaky-crusted pie one of our home economists' favorites. It is completely prepared in the microwave.

COOK'S NOTE
Baking Pies

If your oven browns the edge of the pie crust before the center is done, completely cover the edge with 2-inch strips of foil. If the whole top is overbrowning, loosely drape a sheet of foil over the pie.

CHOCOLATE SILK PECAN PIE

NUTRIENTS PER 1/10 OF RECIPE
Calories	490	Sodium	240mg
Fat	32g	Potassium	180mg
Cholesterol	90mg		

Chocolate Silk Pecan Pie

This luscious pecan pie topped with rich chocolate is one of our favorites. It is important to use the full amount of chocolate chips so the filling sets up properly.

Creamy French Silk Pie

This is a simplified and lighter version of an all-time favorite chocolate pie — without the raw eggs that have become a recent concern. Refrigerated all-ready pie crusts help make the preparation a snap.

CRUST
15-ounce package refrigerated pie crusts
1 teaspoon flour

PECAN MIXTURE
⅓ cup sugar
½ cup dark corn syrup
3 tablespoons margarine or butter, melted
⅛ teaspoon salt, if desired
2 eggs
½ cup chopped pecans

FILLING
1 cup hot milk
¼ teaspoon vanilla
1⅓ cups (8 ounces) semi-sweet chocolate chips

TOPPING
1 cup whipping cream
2 tablespoons powdered sugar
¼ teaspoon vanilla
Chocolate Curls, if desired (See Index)

Prepare pie crust according to package directions for *filled one-crust pie* using 9-inch pie pan. (Refrigerate remaining crust for later use.) Heat oven to 350°F. In small bowl, combine sugar, corn syrup, margarine, salt and eggs; beat 1 minute at medium speed. Stir in pecans. Pour into pie crust-lined pan. Bake at 350°F. for 40 to 55 minutes or until center of pie is puffed and golden brown. Cool 1 hour.

While filled crust is cooling, in blender container or food processor bowl with metal blade, combine all filling ingredients; blend 1 minute or until smooth. Refrigerate about 1½ hours or until mixture is slightly thickened but not set. Gently stir; pour into cooled, filled crust. Refrigerate until firm, about 1 hour.

In small bowl, beat topping ingredients until stiff peaks form. Spoon or pipe over filling. Garnish with Chocolate Curls. Store in refrigerator.
8 to 10 servings.

A MOST REQUESTED RECIPE

CREAMY FRENCH SILK PIE

15-ounce package refrigerated pie crusts
1 teaspoon flour

FILLING
¼ cup sugar
3 tablespoons cornstarch
1½ cups milk
6-ounce package (1 cup) semi-sweet chocolate chips
1 teaspoon vanilla
1½ cups whipping cream
2 tablespoons powdered sugar

Heat oven to 450°F. Prepare pie crust according to package directions for *unfilled one-crust* pie using 9-inch pie pan. (Refrigerate remaining crust for later use.) Bake at 450°F. for 9 to 11 minutes or until light golden brown. Cool completely.

In medium saucepan, combine sugar and cornstarch; blend well. Gradually add milk; cook over medium heat until mixture boils, stirring constantly. Reserve 1 tablespoon of the chocolate chips for topping. Add remaining chocolate chips and vanilla, stirring until melted and smooth. Pour into large mixing bowl; cover surface with plastic wrap. Cool to room temperature.

In large bowl, combine whipping cream and powdered sugar; beat until soft peaks form. Reserve 1½ cups of whipped cream for topping. Beat cooled chocolate mixture at medium speed until light and fluffy, about 1 minute; fold chocolate mixture into remaining whipped cream. Spoon evenly into cooled baked crust. Top with reserved 1½ cups whipped cream. Chop reserved 1 tablespoon chocolate chips; sprinkle over top. Refrigerate 2 to 3 hours before serving. Store in refrigerator. **10 servings.**

NUTRIENTS PER 1/10 OF RECIPE
Calories	370	Sodium	115mg
Fat	26g	Potassium	150mg
Cholesterol	60mg		

Pictured left to right: Linzer Tart, page 74; Mocha Frappe Pie; Chocolate Wedges, page 130

MOCHA FRAPPE PIE

CRUST
- 1 cup all purpose or unbleached flour
- 2 tablespoons sugar
- ½ teaspoon salt
- ⅓ cup shortening
- 1 egg yolk
- 2 to 3 tablespoons water

FILLING
- 4¼ cups miniature marshmallows
- ¼ cup sugar
- 5-ounce can (about ½ cup) evaporated milk
- 2 teaspoons instant coffee granules or crystals
- 6-ounce package (1 cup) semi-sweet chocolate chips
- 1 cup whipping cream, whipped
- Chocolate Curls, if desired (See Index)

Heat oven to 375°F. Lightly spoon flour into measuring cup; level off. In medium bowl, combine flour, 2 tablespoons sugar and salt; mix well. Using pastry blender or fork, cut in shortening until mixture resembles coarse crumbs. In small bowl, combine egg yolk and 2 tablespoons of the water. Stir egg yolk mixture into flour mixture with fork until mixture forms a ball. Add additional water, 1 teaspoon at a time, until dough is just moist enough to hold together.

Shape dough into a ball. Flatten ball; smooth edges. On lightly floured surface, roll lightly from center to edge into 10½-inch circle. Fold dough in half; fit evenly in 9-inch pie pan. Do not stretch. Turn edges under; flute. Prick bottom and sides of pastry generously with fork. Bake at 375°F. for 12 to 17 minutes or until light golden brown. Cool.

In large saucepan over low heat, melt marshmallows with ¼ cup sugar, milk and instant coffee, stirring occasionally until smooth. Stir in chocolate chips until melted. Cool slightly. Spread ¾ cup of chocolate mixture in bottom of cooled baked crust. Refrigerate remaining chocolate mixture 15 minutes or until thoroughly chilled.

Fold whipped cream into remaining chilled chocolate mixture. Spoon over chocolate layer; spread evenly. Refrigerate at least 2 hours before serving. Garnish with Chocolate Curls. Store in refrigerator. **8 servings.**

NUTRIENTS PER 1/8 OF RECIPE

Calories	510	Sodium	180mg
Fat	29g	Potassium	180mg
Cholesterol	80mg		

COOK'S NOTE
Pans for Baking Pies

Use the pan size specified in the recipe so the pastry and filling will fit properly. If you are unsure of a pan's size, measure the top inside diameter.

FROSTY MINT ICE CREAM PIES

CHOCOLATE DATE PECAN PIE

Frosty Mint Ice Cream Pies

There are a variety of mint-flavored ice creams available. Any one of them would be wonderful for this easy make-ahead dessert.

COOK'S NOTE
Cooling Baked Pies

Cool a baked pie on a wire rack. This allows air to circulate underneath the pie, preventing a soggy crust.

---

1 package pudding-included devil's food or dark chocolate cake mix
1 can ready-to-spread chocolate fudge frosting
¾ cup water
6 cups (1½ quarts) mint chocolate chip or favorite flavor ice cream, slightly softened

Heat oven to 350°F. Generously grease bottom, sides and rim of two 9-inch pie pans.* In large bowl, combine cake mix, ¾ cup of the frosting and water. Blend at low speed until moistened; beat 2 minutes at highest speed. Spread half of batter (2¼ cups) in bottom of each greased pan. Do not spread up sides of pan. Bake at 350°F. for 20 to 27 minutes. *Do not overbake.* Cakes will collapse to form shells. Cool completely.

Spoon ice cream evenly into each shell. In small saucepan over low heat, warm remaining frosting until just melted, stirring occasionally. Drop by teaspoonfuls over ice cream; lightly swirl with tip of knife. Freeze until firm. Let stand at room temperature 10 to 15 minutes before serving. **12 servings.**

TIP: *Eight-inch pie pans are not recommended.

HIGH ALTITUDE—Above 3500 Feet: Add ¼ cup flour to dry cake mix. Bake as directed above.

NUTRIENTS PER 1/12 OF RECIPE

Calories	460	Sodium	490mg
Fat	17g	Potassium	350mg
Cholesterol	28mg		

CRUST
15-ounce package refrigerated pie crusts
1 teaspoon flour

FILLING
½ cup all purpose or unbleached flour
1 cup firmly packed brown sugar
½ cup butter or margarine, softened
1 teaspoon vanilla
2 eggs
6-ounce package (1 cup) semi-sweet chocolate chips
1 cup chopped pecans
1 cup chopped dates
Whipped cream, if desired

Prepare pie crust according to package directions for *filled one-crust pie* using 9-inch pie pan. (Refrigerate remaining crust for later use.) Heat oven to 325°F.

Lightly spoon flour into measuring cup; level off. In large bowl, combine ½ cup flour, brown sugar, butter, vanilla and eggs; beat well. Stir in chocolate chips, pecans and dates. Spread evenly in pie crust-lined pan. Bake at 325°F. for 55 to 60 minutes or until deep golden brown. Serve warm with whipped cream. Garnish as desired. Store in refrigerator. **10 servings.**

TIP: Cover edge of pie crust with strip of foil during last 15 to 20 minutes of baking if necessary to prevent excessive browning.

NUTRIENTS PER 1/10 OF RECIPE

Calories	590	Sodium	210mg
Fat	36g	Potassium	340mg
Cholesterol	110mg		

Banana Split Pie

BANANA SPLIT PIE

1 medium banana, thinly sliced
2 teaspoons lemon juice
1 quart (4 cups) strawberry ice cream
9-inch prepared chocolate crumb crust
½ cup chocolate fudge ice cream topping
½ cup pineapple ice cream topping
2 tablespoons chopped pecans

In small bowl, gently toss banana slices in lemon juice; set aside. Spoon half of the ice cream into prepared crust; arrange banana slices over ice cream. Drizzle fudge topping over bananas; spoon on remaining ice cream. Drizzle pineapple topping over top; sprinkle evenly with pecans. Freeze until firm, at least 6 hours. About 30 minutes before serving, place in refrigerator to thaw slightly. **8 servings.**

NUTRIENTS PER 1/8 OF RECIPE

Calories	420	Sodium	180mg
Fat	20g	Potassium	270mg
Cholesterol	37mg		

Banana Split Pie

It is easier to fill this pie with ice cream that is slightly softened. To soften one quart in the microwave, open the ice cream container and microwave on MEDIUM for 20 to 40 seconds. Add time as needed in 10 second intervals.

CHOCOLATE COVERED CHERRY TART

15-ounce package refrigerated pie crusts
1 teaspoon flour
21-ounce can cherry fruit pie filling

GLAZE
½ cup semi-sweet chocolate chips
3 tablespoons milk
¼ teaspoon vanilla
Sliced almonds

Heat oven to 400°F. Prepare first pie crust according to package directions for *two-crust pie* using 9-inch tart pan with removable bottom. Do not trim crust. Spoon pie filling into crust; do not allow filling to touch untrimmed edge of crust. Unfold second crust; remove plastic sheets. Press out fold lines. From second crust, cut 9-inch circle; cut 3 slits for steam to escape. Place over filling. Brush untrimmed edges of bottom crust with water. Bring edges over 9-inch circle; press lightly to seal. Bake at 400°F. for 45 to 50 minutes or until deep golden brown. Cool completely in pan.

Invert tart onto serving plate. (Allow to remain upside down.) Remove pan sides and bottom. In small saucepan over low heat, melt chocolate chips with milk, stirring constantly until smooth. Stir in vanilla. Spread over tart, allowing some to run down sides. Garnish with sliced almonds. To serve, cut into wedges. Store in refrigerator.
12 servings.

NUTRIENTS PER 1/12 OF RECIPE

Calories	310	Sodium	220mg
Fat	14g	Potassium	90mg
Cholesterol	10mg		

CHOCOLATE TART SHELLS

8 ounces (8 squares) semi-sweet chocolate, cut into pieces
2 tablespoons shortening

Line 8 muffin cups with foil or paper baking cups. In small saucepan over low heat, melt chocolate and shortening, stirring constantly until smooth. Remove from heat. Using flat brush, brush insides of foil-lined muffin cups with melted chocolate until about ⅛ inch thick. Refrigerate cups 5 to 10 minutes or until chocolate is set. Brush second layer of chocolate over first layer. Refrigerate until chocolate is set. Remove from muffin cups and carefully peel foil away from chocolate tart shells. Store in refrigerator or freezer until ready to use. To serve, fill with your favorite mousse, ice cream or fresh fruit.
8 to 9 shells.

NUTRIENTS PER 1 SHELL

Calories	160	Sodium	0mg
Fat	12g	Potassium	80mg
Cholesterol	0mg		

LINZER TART

¾ cup all purpose or unbleached flour
⅓ cup sugar
¾ cup (15 wafers) crushed chocolate cookie wafers
¼ teaspoon cinnamon
2½-ounce package hazelnuts (filberts), ground (about ¾ cup)
¾ cup unsalted butter, salted butter or margarine, cut into pieces, softened
1 egg yolk
1 cup seedless raspberry jam
Whipped cream

Heat oven to 350°F. Lightly spoon flour into measuring cup; level off. In large bowl, combine flour, sugar, cookie crumbs, cinnamon and hazelnuts. Stir in butter and egg yolk; blend well. Press dough in bottom and 1 inch up sides of 9½-inch tart pan with removable bottom. Bake at 350°F. for 15 to 20 minutes or until top becomes dull and edges start to pull away from sides of pan. (Crust puffs in oven and falls when removed from oven.) Cool. Spread jam over center of cooled baked crust. Pipe or spoon whipped cream in lattice pattern over jam. Store in refrigerator.
16 servings.

HIGH ALTITUDE—Above 3500 Feet: No change.

NUTRIENTS PER 1/16 OF RECIPE

Calories	250	Sodium	15mg
Fat	15g	Potassium	60mg
Cholesterol	52mg		

Linzer Tart

This chocolate-raspberry sensation is very easy to prepare. It can be made up to twenty-four hours in advance and stored in the refrigerator until serving time.

Chocolate Tart Shells

These impressive tart shells are not difficult to make. For variety, make them with white chocolate or almond bark.

SPIRAL CHOCOLATE JAM TART

CRUST
- **15-ounce package refrigerated pie crusts**
- **1 teaspoon flour**

FILLING
- **¼ cup sugar**
- **¾ cup whipping cream**
- **4 egg yolks**
- **6 ounces (6 squares) semi-sweet chocolate, chopped**
- **2 tablespoons butter or margarine, softened**
- **1 tablespoon vanilla**
- **½ cup apricot, strawberry or raspberry jam**
- **2 ounces (2 squares) white baking bar or vanilla-flavored candy coating**

Heat oven to 450°F. Prepare pie crust according to package directions for *unfilled one-crust pie* using 10-inch tart pan with removable bottom. (Refrigerate remaining crust for later use.) Place prepared crust in pan; press in bottom and up sides of pan. Trim edges if necessary. Generously prick crust with fork. Bake at 450°F. for 9 to 11 minutes or until golden brown. Cool.

In small saucepan, combine sugar, whipping cream and egg yolks. Cook over low heat about 5 to 10 minutes or until mixture begins to thicken, stirring constantly. Remove from heat. Stir in semi-sweet chocolate, butter and vanilla; blend until smooth. Cool slightly. Spread jam over cooled baked crust. Spread chocolate mixture over jam layer.

In small saucepan over low heat, melt white baking bar, stirring constantly until smooth. Cool slightly. Spoon melted white baking bar into pastry bag fitted with writing tip. Starting from center of tart and working outward, pipe a spiral pattern over top of tart. Working from center of spiral to outer edges, draw blade of small knife lightly through spiral. Frequently wipe knife clean to ensure a clean design. Garnish as desired. Store in refrigerator.
16 servings.

NUTRIENTS PER 1/16 OF RECIPE

Calories	250	Sodium	105mg
Fat	16g	Potassium	75mg
Cholesterol	90mg		

Spiral Chocolate Jam Tart

This dessert is a show-stopper! It can be made with any flavor of jam you have on hand. Follow the easy directions for making the unique spiral design.

Derby Day Tart; Chocolate-Dipped Nuts, page 134

DERBY DAY TART

CRUST
    15-ounce package refrigerated pie crusts
    1 teaspoon flour

FILLING
    3 eggs
    1 cup firmly packed brown sugar
    ¼ cup all purpose or unbleached flour
    ¼ cup margarine or butter, melted
    2 tablespoons bourbon
    ½ teaspoon vanilla
    ¾ cup semi-sweet chocolate chips
    1 cup chopped pecans

TOPPING
    ¼ cup semi-sweet chocolate chips
    ½ cup whipping cream
    2 tablespoons powdered sugar
    2 teaspoons bourbon
    Chocolate-Dipped Nuts, if desired (See Index)

Heat oven to 450°F. Prepare pie crust according to package directions for *unfilled one-crust pie* using 10-inch tart pan with removable bottom. (Refrigerate remaining crust for later use.) Place prepared crust in pan; press in bottom and up sides of pan. Trim edges if necessary. Generously prick crust with fork. Bake at 450°F. for 9 to 11 minutes or until golden brown. Cool. Reduce oven temperature to 350°F.

In small bowl, beat eggs until well blended. Add brown sugar, ¼ cup flour, margarine, 2 tablespoons bourbon and vanilla; beat until well blended. Stir in ¾ cup chocolate chips and pecans. Pour into cooled baked crust. Bake at 350°F. for 25 to 30 minutes or until filling is set. Cool.

In small saucepan over low heat, melt ¼ cup chocolate chips, stirring constantly until smooth. Drizzle over pie. Refrigerate until serving time. Just before serving, beat whipping cream with powdered sugar and 2 teaspoons bourbon until stiff peaks form. Top tart with whipped cream. Garnish with Chocolate-Dipped Nuts. Store in refrigerator. **8 to 10 servings.**

Derby Day Tart

This tart is an adaptation of a pie traditionally served on Kentucky Derby Day. The tempting trio of chocolate, caramel and pecans is irresistible.

NUTRIENTS PER 1/10 OF RECIPE

Calories	510	Sodium	220mg
Fat	33g	Potassium	230mg
Cholesterol	100mg		

CHOCOLATE CARAMEL ALMOND TART

CRUST
15-ounce package refrigerated pie
    crusts
1 teaspoon flour

FILLING
20 vanilla caramels, unwrapped
3 tablespoons whipping cream
3 tablespoons butter or margarine
1 cup sifted powdered sugar
¾ cup chopped almonds, toasted*
    or unsalted dry roasted peanuts

GLAZE
⅔ cup whipping cream
5 ounces (5 squares) semi-sweet
    chocolate, cut up

TOPPING
1 cup whipping cream
2 tablespoons powdered sugar
¼ teaspoon vanilla
Toasted almonds*

Heat oven to 450°F. Prepare pie crust according to package directions for *unfilled one-crust pie* using 9-inch tart pan with removable bottom or 9-inch pie pan. (Refrigerate remaining crust for later use.) Place prepared crust in pan; press in bottom and up sides of pan. Along top edge, fold excess dough back into pan to form double-thick sides; gently press against sides of pan. Generously prick crust with fork. Bake at 450°F. for 9 to 11 minutes or until golden brown. Cool completely.

In small heavy saucepan over low heat, combine caramels, 3 tablespoons whipping cream and butter; cook until caramels and butter are melted, stirring occasionally. Remove from heat. Beat in 1 cup powdered sugar until well blended. Stir in ¾ cup almonds. *Immediately* spread in bottom of cooled baked crust. In another small saucepan over low heat, melt glaze ingredients, stirring constantly until smooth. Pour over caramel mixture. Refrigerate until firm, about 2 hours.

In small bowl, beat 1 cup whipping cream with 2 tablespoons powdered sugar and vanilla until stiff peaks form. Spread ½ of whipped cream mixture over chilled filling. With pastry bag fitted with tip or small spoon, use remaining whipped cream mixture to make decorative border. Sprinkle with toasted almonds. Refrigerate until serving time. (If tart has been refrigerated for more than 4 hours, remove 30 minutes before serving.) Store in refrigerator. **10 to 12 servings.**

TIP: *To toast almonds, spread on cookie sheet; bake at 375°F. for 5 to 10 minutes or until golden brown, stirring occasionally. Or spread in thin layer in microwave-safe pie pan. Microwave on HIGH for 3 to 4 minutes or until light golden brown, stirring frequently.

NUTRIENTS PER 1/12 OF RECIPE

Calories	470	Sodium	190mg
Fat	33g	Potassium	190mg
Cholesterol	60mg		

CANNOLI STRAWBERRY TARTS

1 cup ricotta cheese
1 cup frozen whipped topping,
    thawed
¼ to ½ teaspoon rum extract
⅓ cup miniature semi-sweet
    chocolate chips
¼ cup powdered sugar
6 individual graham cracker tart
    shells
6 large strawberries, sliced

In medium bowl, combine ricotta cheese, whipped topping, rum extract, chocolate chips and powdered sugar; blend well. Spoon about ⅓ cup of ricotta cheese mixture into each tart shell. Arrange strawberry slices on top of each tart. Serve immediately or refrigerate until serving time. **6 servings.**

NUTRIENTS PER 1/6 OF RECIPE

Calories	280	Sodium	160mg
Fat	16g	Potassium	150mg
Cholesterol	10mg		

Chocolate Caramel Almond Tart

This delectable tart is reminiscent of Almond Roca Candy. Topped with whipped cream, it is irresistible.

Cannoli Strawberry Tarts

These are wonderful little tarts with a traditional Italian cheese filling. They are great for a special occasion. Top them with sliced berries or strawberry fans. To make fans, select firm berries with stems. Starting at the tip, cut 4 to 5 slices almost to stem. Spread slices to form the fan.

CRANBERRY CHOCOLATE TART

CRUST

15-ounce package refrigerated pie crusts
1 teaspoon flour
½ cup semi-sweet chocolate chips
¼ cup half-and-half

FILLING

1 cup dairy sour cream
¾ cup milk
1 tablespoon grated orange peel
3½-ounce package instant vanilla pudding and pie filling mix

TOPPING

16-ounce can whole cranberry sauce

Heat oven to 450°F. Prepare pie crust according to package directions for *unfilled one-crust pie* using 10-inch tart pan with removable bottom. (Refrigerate remaining crust for later use.) Place prepared crust in pan; press in bottom and up sides of pan. Trim edges if necessary. Generously prick crust with fork. Bake at 450°F. for 9 to 11 minutes or until golden brown. In small saucepan over low heat, melt chocolate chips with half-and-half, stirring constantly until smooth. Spread chocolate mixture in bottom of baked crust. Cool. Refrigerate until chocolate is firm.

In small bowl, combine all filling ingredients. Beat 1 minute at low speed or until blended; let stand 5 minutes. Pour filling over chocolate layer; spread evenly.

Place cranberry sauce in small bowl; stir gently. Spoon sauce over filling, covering completely. Refrigerate at least 1 hour. Let stand at room temperature 10 minutes before serving. Store in refrigerator. **10 servings.**

NUTRIENTS PER 1/10 OF RECIPE

Calories	320	Sodium	210mg
Fat	16g	Potassium	130mg
Cholesterol	15mg		

CHOCOLATE TOFFEE CLOUD

MERINGUE

6 egg whites
½ teaspoon cream of tartar
Dash salt
2 cups sugar

FILLING

2 cups whipping cream
½ cup powdered sugar
⅓ cup unsweetened cocoa
½ cup coarsely crushed toffee candy bars, reserving 3 tablespoons for garnish

Heat oven to 275°F. Line 2 cookie sheets with parchment or brown paper. In large bowl, combine egg whites, cream of tartar and salt; beat until foamy. Gradually add sugar; beat until stiff peaks form. *Do not underbeat.* Spread half of mixture to an 8-inch circle on parchment paper-lined cookie sheet; repeat with remaining mixture on second cookie sheet. Bake at 275°F. for 50 to 60 minutes or until crisp and very light golden brown around edges. Turn oven off; let stand in closed oven for 2 hours. Remove meringues from oven. Cool completely. Remove from parchment paper.

In medium bowl, beat whipping cream, powdered sugar and cocoa until stiff peaks form. Fold in crushed candy. To assemble, place one meringue layer on serving plate. Spread with half of filling. Repeat layers with remaining meringue and filling, ending with filling. Sprinkle with reserved 3 tablespoons crushed candy. Refrigerate several hours before serving. Store in refrigerator. **12 to 16 servings.**

NUTRIENTS PER 1/16 OF RECIPE

Calories	260	Sodium	65mg
Fat	14g	Potassium	60mg
Cholesterol	41mg		

COOK'S NOTE
Making Meringues

Even before the eggbeater was invented in 1870, meringue tarts and crusts were popular. For a successful meringue crust, it is important to beat the sugar in gradually and to allow the standing time in the oven after baking. Add the sugar one tablespoon at a time while beating the egg whites. Bake the meringue shells in a slow oven so they remain white and become dry. Store baked meringue tightly covered to maintain the crisp quality and prevent toughening. To achieve that light crispness, it is best to make meringues on a day when the humidity is low.

Fruit-Filled Chocolate Meringues

FRUIT-FILLED CHOCOLATE MERINGUES

MERINGUES
  2 egg whites
  ¼ teaspoon salt
  ¼ teaspoon vinegar
  ½ cup sugar
  ½ teaspoon vanilla
  1 tablespoon unsweetened cocoa

FILLING
  1 to 1½ cups assorted fresh fruits
  Fudge sauce, if desired

Heat oven to 275°F. Line cookie sheet with parchment or brown paper. In small bowl, combine egg whites, salt and vinegar; beat until foamy. Gradually add sugar and vanilla, beating until stiff peaks form. Sift cocoa over beaten egg whites; fold into mixture.

Using a heaping tablespoonful of egg white mixture, drop 6 individual mounds of mixture onto parchment paper-lined cookie sheet. Make a deep well in center of each, spreading egg white mixture to a 3-inch circle. Bake at 275°F. for 45 minutes or until crisp. Turn oven off; leave meringues in closed oven for 1½ hours. Remove from oven. Cool completely. Remove from parchment paper. Just before serving, fill meringues with fresh fruit. Serve with fudge sauce. **6 servings.**

NUTRIENTS PER 1/6 OF RECIPE

Calories	150	Sodium	135mg
Fat	0g	Potassium	130mg
Cholesterol	0mg		

Fruit-Filled
Chocolate
Meringues

Suggestions for fresh fruit to serve in meringues include sliced peaches, strawberries, blueberries, grapes, kiwifruit, raspberries, nectarines and oranges. Prepared with egg whites, baked meringue is a low-cholesteral, low-fat treat. To keep calories down too, serve without the fudge sauce.

Creamy Chocolate Mousse, page 92; Chocolate Seashells, page 126

Frozen & Refrigerated Desserts

Smooth and frosty. Cool and refreshing. These recipes are impressive in appearance and taste, but just as remarkable is their ease of preparation, whether it's a special treat to charm the kids or a fabulous dinner party finale.

These frozen and refrigerated delights can be made ahead and stored until serving time with little or no last-minute work. Among the most glamorous is White Chocolate Mousse with Raspberry. Both the mousse and the raspberry sauce can be made ahead. At serving time, the milk chocolate glaze is prepared and the dessert is assembled. The results: glorious!

Many recipes in this collection use few ingredients. Creamy Chocolate Mousse is made without eggs and calls for just three ingredients — whipped cream, sweet cooking chocolate and vanilla. Be sure to stir constantly when melting this and all other chocolate mixtures. A number of these chocolaty desserts capitalize on the convenience of products like instant pudding and pie filling mix, frozen whipped topping and frozen fruits. Others are made with ingredients you probably have on hand most of the time.

Cheesecakes feed the richest fantasies of dessert devotees. Unfortunately, their glamorous gourmet qualities often intimidate the best of good cooks. However, the preparation is really quite simple. You may want to start with light and easy no-bake Double Chocolate Cheesecake. Then move on to the traditional recipes that call for baking.

You'll find single-serving delights as well as recipes to serve a crowd — in a multitude of shapes, colors and tastes. Chocolate is teamed with cream cheese, marshmallows, nuts and candies. It's gently enhanced with the flavors of mint and rum extract as well as fruity liqueurs and juices. We think you'll agree that one of the best flavor combinations is chocolate and coffee. Keep Creamy Mocha Frozen Dessert on hand for unexpected guests. And as a real show-stopper, serve meringue-topped Coffee Toffee Alaska Pie.

FROZEN RASPBERRY MACADAMIA DESSERT

CREAMY MOCHA FROZEN DESSERT

Creamy Mocha Frozen Dessert

For easier serving, allow this dessert to thaw in the refrigerator for 15 to 20 minutes before cutting it.

FROZEN RASPBERRY MACADAMIA DESSERT

CRUST

- 1 cup (20 wafers) crushed vanilla wafers
- ½ cup finely chopped macadamia nuts or almonds
- ¼ cup margarine or butter, melted

FILLING

- 14-ounce can sweetened condensed milk (not evaporated)
- 3 tablespoons lemon juice
- 3 tablespoons orange-flavored liqueur or orange juice
- 10-ounce package frozen raspberries with syrup, thawed
- 1 cup whipping cream, whipped

  Chocolate Filigree Hearts (See Index)

Heat oven to 375°F. In small bowl, combine all crust ingredients; blend well. Press firmly in bottom of ungreased 8-inch springform pan. Bake at 375°F. for 8 to 10 minutes. Cool.

In large bowl, combine sweetened condensed milk, lemon juice and liqueur; beat until smooth. Add raspberries; beat at low speed until well blended. Fold in whipped cream. Pour over cooled baked crust. Freeze until firm. Let stand 15 minutes at room temperature before serving. Garnish with Chocolate Filigree Hearts. **12 servings.**

NUTRIENTS PER 1/12 OF RECIPE

Calories	390	Sodium	130mg
Fat	22g	Potassium	250mg
Cholesterol	45mg		

CREAMY MOCHA FROZEN DESSERT

CRUST

- 1 cup (20 wafers) crushed chocolate cookie wafers
- ½ cup finely chopped pecans
- ¼ cup margarine or butter, melted

FILLING

- 2 (8-ounce) packages cream cheese, softened
- 14-ounce can sweetened condensed milk (not evaporated)
- ½ cup chocolate-flavored syrup
- 2 teaspoons instant coffee granules or crystals
- 1 tablespoon water
- 8-ounce container frozen whipped topping, thawed
- ¼ cup chopped pecans

In medium bowl, combine all crust ingredients; blend well. Press firmly in bottom of ungreased 13 × 9-inch pan or 10-inch springform pan.

In large bowl, beat cream cheese until fluffy. Add sweetened condensed milk and chocolate syrup; beat until smooth. In small bowl, combine instant coffee and water; stir until dissolved. Stir into cream cheese mixture. Fold in whipped topping. Spoon into crust-lined pan. Sprinkle evenly with ¼ cup pecans. Freeze until firm. **16 servings.**

NUTRIENTS PER 1/16 OF RECIPE

Calories	370	Sodium	180mg
Fat	24g	Potassium	220mg
Cholesterol	45mg		

Creamy Mocha Frozen Dessert

GOURMET CHOCOLATE CHIP ICE CREAM

CHOCOLATE ICE CREAM CAKE ROLLS

Chocolate Ice Cream Cake Rolls

For variety, each cake roll can be filled with a different flavor of ice cream. How about mint, toasted almond fudge or cherry nut? Make these ahead and store them in the freezer for those unexpected occasions that warrant something special.

COOK'S NOTE
Making Ice Cream

When using a new coolant-type ice cream freezer, we recommend reading the manufacturer's directions in advance. For best results, be sure to prepare the custard mixture one day ahead. Many manufacturers also recommend that the coolant cylinder be placed in a freezer compartment overnight.

1 cup sugar
2 cups half-and-half
4 ounces (4 squares) unsweetened chocolate, cut into pieces, melted
2 eggs
2 cups whipping cream
2 teaspoons vanilla
½ cup vanilla milk chips, finely chopped
½ cup macadamia nuts, finely chopped, if desired

In medium saucepan, combine sugar, half-and-half, melted chocolate and eggs; blend well. Stirring constantly, cook over medium heat until mixture is slightly thickened and coats a metal spoon. *Do not boil.* Cool, cover and refrigerate up to 1 day. Add whipping cream and vanilla; blend well. Refrigerate until ready to freeze. Prepare ice cream freezer according to manufacturer's directions; freeze as directed. Add vanilla chips and nuts during last 5 minutes of freezing process.
12 (½-cup) servings.

MICROWAVE DIRECTIONS:
In 8-cup microwave-safe measuring cup, microwave chocolate on MEDIUM for 3½ to 4 minutes or until melted, stirring once halfway through cooking. Stir in sugar and eggs. In 4-cup microwave-safe measuring cup, microwave half-and-half on HIGH for 2 to 2½ minutes or until very warm. Using wire whisk, gradually beat warm half-and-half into chocolate mixture. Microwave on MEDIUM for 9 to 12 minutes or until mixture is slightly thickened and coats a metal spoon, stirring every 2 minutes. *Do not boil.* (If mixture begins to curdle, beat vigorously with wire whisk.) Cool, cover and refrigerate up to 1 day. Continue as directed above.

NUTRIENTS PER 1/12 OF RECIPE

Calories	400	Sodium	50mg
Fat	31g	Potassium	210mg
Cholesterol	120mg		

Powdered sugar
4 eggs
½ cup water
1 package pudding-included devil's food cake mix
2 quarts (8 cups) any flavor ice cream, softened
Fudge or any flavor ice cream topping

Heat oven to 350°F. Grease two 15 × 10 × 1-inch baking pans; line with waxed paper and grease again.* Generously sprinkle 2 clean towels with powdered sugar. In large bowl, beat eggs at high speed for 5 minutes or until thick and lemon-colored. Reduce speed to low; add water. Gradually add cake mix; blend until dry ingredients are moistened. Beat 2 minutes at high speed. Spread half of batter in each greased, waxed paper-lined pan. Bake 1 at a time at 350°F. for 14 to 20 minutes or until top springs back when touched lightly in center.* *Do not overbake.* Immediately invert cake onto powdered-sugared towel. Carefully remove waxed paper. Starting at shortest sides, roll up cake in towel. Cool completely.

Carefully unroll cooled cake. Remove towel. Spread each cake with 1 quart ice cream; roll up loosely. Wrap each in foil; freeze until firm. To serve, cut into 1-inch slices; drizzle with fudge topping. Store in freezer.
2 cake rolls; 10 servings each.

TIP: *If only one 15 × 10 × 1-inch baking pan is available, set half of batter aside. Bake as directed immediately after first cake is removed from pan.

HIGH ALTITUDE – Above 3500 Feet: No change.

NUTRIENTS PER 1/20 OF RECIPE

Calories	300	Sodium	290mg
Fat	12g	Potassium	230mg
Cholesterol	79mg		

Chocolate Ice Cream Cake Rolls

COFFEE TOFFEE ALASKA PIE

CRUST
1¼ cups (25 wafers) crushed
    chocolate cookie wafers
¼ cup margarine or butter, melted

FILLING
1 pint (2 cups) coffee ice cream,
    slightly softened
¼ cup chocolate-flavored syrup
4 (1⅛-ounce) toffee candy bars,
    crushed
1 pint (2 cups) chocolate ice
    cream, slightly softened

MERINGUE
5 egg whites
¼ teaspoon cream of tartar
⅔ cup sugar

In medium bowl, combine cookie crumbs and margarine; blend well. Press in bottom and up sides of 9-inch pie pan. Freeze for 15 minutes.

Spoon coffee ice cream into chilled crust. Drizzle with chocolate syrup; sprinkle with ½ of the crushed candy. Freeze for 15 minutes. Spoon chocolate ice cream over candy; sprinkle with remaining crushed candy. Freeze until very firm.

Heat oven to 450°F. In small bowl, beat egg whites with cream of tartar until soft peaks form. Add sugar 1 tablespoon at a time, beating until stiff peaks form. Spread about ⅓ of meringue over pie, sealing to edge of crust. With pastry bag fitted with large star tip or with spoon, swirl remaining meringue over pie.

Bake at 450°F. for 2 to 3 minutes or until lightly browned. Return to freezer; freeze several hours or until firm. Let stand 5 to 10 minutes at room temperature before serving. **8 servings.**

NUTRIENTS PER 1/8 OF RECIPE

Calories	470	Sodium	230mg
Fat	25g	Potassium	230mg
Cholesterol	36mg		

FROZEN CHOCOLATE MINT SQUARES

CRUST
2 cups (40 wafers) crushed vanilla
    wafers
¼ cup margarine or butter, melted

FILLING
½ cup margarine or butter,
    softened
1½ cups powdered sugar
1 teaspoon vanilla
3 ounces (3 squares) unsweetened
    chocolate, melted, cooled
12-ounce container frozen whipped
    topping, thawed
3 cups miniature marshmallows
½ cup (about 24 candies) finely
    crushed hard peppermint candy
Grated Chocolate, if desired
    (See Index)

In medium bowl, combine crust ingredients; blend well. Press in bottom of ungreased 13×9-inch pan. In small bowl, combine ½ cup margarine, powdered sugar and vanilla; beat until light and fluffy. Add melted chocolate; beat well. Stir in 1½ cups of the whipped topping; spread over crust. In medium bowl, combine marshmallows, peppermint candy and remaining whipped topping; blend well. Spread over chocolate layer. Sprinkle with Grated Chocolate. Freeze until firm. Let stand 15 minutes at room temperature before serving. **16 servings.**

NUTRIENTS PER 1/16 OF RECIPE

Calories	320	Sodium	140mg
Fat	19g	Potassium	65mg
Cholesterol	4mg		

Frozen Chocolate Mint Squares

This sweet and chocolaty dessert can be made up to one month in advance of the serving occasion. Candy canes can be substituted for the peppermint candies.

COOK'S NOTE
Storing Ice Cream

Store an ice cream or frozen dessert at about 0°F. in a tightly covered container with little air space between the dessert and the lid. Plastic wrap can be placed directly on the surface of the dessert or under the lid, if desired.

CHOCOLATE-CHERRY ICE CREAM DESSERT

BASE
2½ cups (30 cookies) finely crushed creme-filled chocolate sandwich cookies

¼ cup margarine or butter, melted

FILLING
½ gallon (8 cups) vanilla ice cream or ice milk, slightly softened

21-ounce can cherry fruit pie filling

Reserve ¼ cup of the crushed cookies for topping. In large bowl, combine remaining 2¼ cups crushed cookies and margarine; blend well. Press lightly in bottom of ungreased 13 × 9-inch pan. Refrigerate 10 to 15 minutes.

Spoon half of the ice cream over chilled base. Spoon pie filling over ice cream. Top pie filling with remaining ice cream; sprinkle with reserved ¼ cup crushed cookies. Freeze at least 2 hours or until firm. Let stand at room temperature 10 to 15 minutes before serving. **15 servings.**

NUTRIENTS PER 1/15 OF RECIPE

Calories	350	Sodium	200mg
Fat	15g	Potassium	180mg
Cholesterol	40mg		

TOFFEE CRUNCH PARFAITS

1 quart (4 cups) coffee or vanilla ice cream, slightly softened

⅓ cup chocolate-flavored syrup

4 (1⅛-ounce) toffee candy bars, crushed

¼ cup whipping cream, whipped, sweetened

In 6 parfait glasses, layer ice cream, chocolate syrup and crushed candy. Freeze until firm. Before serving, let stand at room temperature 5 to 10 minutes. Top with whipped cream. Garnish as desired. **6 servings.**

NUTRIENTS PER 1/6 OF RECIPE

Calories	390	Sodium	150mg
Fat	25g	Potassium	250mg
Cholesterol	53mg		

PEANUT CHOCOLATE PARFAIT DESSERT

BASE
1 package pudding-included devil's food cake mix

½ cup margarine or butter, melted

¼ cup milk

1 egg

¾ cup peanuts

FILLING
1½ cups powdered sugar

¾ cup peanut butter

8-ounce package cream cheese, softened

2¼ cups milk

8-ounce container frozen whipped topping, thawed

5¼-ounce package instant vanilla pudding and pie filling mix (6-serving size)

TOPPING
½ cup peanuts

1.45-ounce bar milk chocolate, chilled, grated

Heat oven to 350°F. Grease and flour bottom only of 13 × 9-inch pan. In large bowl, combine all base ingredients except ¾ cup peanuts; beat at medium speed until well blended. By hand, stir in ¾ cup peanuts. Spread evenly in greased and floured pan. Bake at 350°F. for 20 to 25 minutes. *Do not overbake.* Cool completely.

In small bowl, combine powdered sugar and peanut butter at low speed until crumbly; set aside. In large bowl, beat cream cheese until smooth. Add milk, whipped topping and pudding mix; beat 2 minutes at low speed until well blended. Pour half of cream cheese mixture over cooled base; spread evenly. Sprinkle with half of peanut butter mixture. Repeat layers with remaining cream cheese and peanut butter mixtures. Sprinkle with ½ cup peanuts; gently press into filling. Sprinkle with grated chocolate. Cover; refrigerate or freeze until serving time. Store in refrigerator or freezer. **16 servings.**

NUTRIENTS PER 1/16 OF RECIPE

Calories	540	Sodium	500mg
Fat	32g	Potassium	330mg
Cholesterol	35mg		

Toffee Crunch Parfaits

Parfait is a French name given to a dessert with alternating layers of ice cream and compatible ingredients. Parfaits can be served in assorted tall, clear glasses.

FUDGY SHERBET PIE

1 cup crisp rice cereal
½ cup chopped nuts
1 can ready-to-spread chocolate fudge frosting
1 quart (4 cups) orange sherbet, softened

Fudgy Sherbet Pie

Crisp rice cereal and nuts are folded into fudge frosting to make the crust for this sherbet pie. Miniature chocolate chips make an ideal topping.

Brush 9-inch pie pan with oil. In large bowl, combine cereal, nuts and frosting; blend until cereal is well coated. Press mixture in bottom and up sides of oiled pan. Freeze about 30 minutes or until slightly firm. Spoon sherbet into crust. Freeze until firm. Let stand at room temperature about 5 minutes before serving. **8 servings.**

NUTRIENTS PER 1/8 OF RECIPE
Calories	430	Sodium	210mg
Fat	16g	Potassium	280mg
Cholesterol	6mg		

Carousel Sundae Cups

Children will love this whimsical dessert. The frosted sponge cake cups can be stored in a covered container until it's time to complete them for birthday party treats.

CREAMY CHOCOLATE PUDDING

¾ cup sugar
⅓ cup unsweetened cocoa
2 tablespoons cornstarch
Dash salt
2 cups milk
2 tablespoons margarine or butter
1 teaspoon vanilla
Whipped cream, if desired
Chocolate Cutouts, if desired (See Index)

In medium saucepan, combine sugar, cocoa, cornstarch and salt; blend well. Stir in milk. Cook over medium heat until mixture comes to a boil, stirring constantly. Cook 1 minute, stirring constantly. Remove from heat. Stir in margarine and vanilla. Pour into individual serving dishes or small serving bowl. Cover surface with plastic wrap; refrigerate until serving time. Garnish with whipped cream and Chocolate Cutouts. **5 (½-cup) servings.**

MICROWAVE DIRECTIONS:
In medium-sized microwave-safe bowl, combine sugar, cocoa, cornstarch, salt and milk; blend well. Microwave on HIGH for 5½ to 6½ minutes or until mixture comes to a boil, beating well with wire whisk twice during cooking. Microwave on HIGH for 1 minute; beat well. Stir in margarine and vanilla. Cover surface with plastic wrap; refrigerate until serving time. Garnish with whipped cream and Chocolate Cutouts.

NUTRIENTS PER 1/5 OF RECIPE
Calories	300	Sodium	170mg
Fat	12g	Potassium	210mg
Cholesterol	18mg		

CAROUSEL SUNDAE CUPS

1 can ready-to-spread chocolate fudge or milk chocolate frosting
16 individual sponge cake cups
48 to 80 animal crackers*
½ gallon (8 cups) any flavor ice cream
Assorted ice cream toppings
Whipped cream or topping
Maraschino cherries

Line cookie sheets with waxed paper. Spread top and sides of each cake cup with frosting. Press 3 to 5 animal crackers into frosting around sides of each cake cup. To assemble sundaes, place frosted cake cups on individual dessert plates. Fill center of each cake cup with scoop of ice cream. Top with ice cream topping, whipped cream and cherry. **16 servings.**

TIP: *An 11-ounce package of animal crackers contains approximately 140 crackers.

NUTRIENTS PER 1/16 OF RECIPE
Calories	520	Sodium	260mg
Fat	20g	Potassium	260mg
Cholesterol	140mg		

Carousel Sundae Cups

Cookies 'n Cream Wedges; Chocolate Cutouts, page 130

COOKIES 'N CREAM WEDGES

COOK'S NOTE
Crushing Cookies

To crush sandwich cookies easily, place them in a plastic bag and press them with a rolling pin.

CRUST
  2 cups (24 cookies) finely crushed creme-filled chocolate sandwich cookies
  ⅓ cup margarine or butter, melted

FILLING
  2 (8-ounce) packages cream cheese, softened
  ⅔ cup sugar
  1 tablespoon vanilla
  1 cup whipping cream, whipped
  2 ounces (2 squares) semi-sweet chocolate, grated

  Chocolate Cutouts (See Index)

In large bowl, combine crust ingredients; blend well. Press in bottom and up sides of ungreased 9-inch springform pan. Refrigerate.

In large bowl, beat cream cheese until fluffy. Gradually add sugar and vanilla; blend well. Fold in whipped cream and grated chocolate. Spoon into chilled crust. Refrigerate at least 2 hours before serving. With small, sharp knife, loosen crust from sides of pan. Remove sides of pan. To serve, cut into wedges. Garnish with Chocolate Cutouts. Store in refrigerator. **16 servings.**

NUTRIENTS PER 1/16 OF RECIPE

Calories	300	Sodium	200mg
Fat	23g	Potassium	65mg
Cholesterol	60mg		

CHOCOLATE RASPBERRY PARFAITS

1 ounce (1 square) unsweetened chocolate
½ cup milk
10-ounce package (40) large marshmallows
⅓ cup black raspberry-flavored liqueur
1 cup whipping cream, whipped
Fresh raspberries

In large saucepan over low heat, melt chocolate with milk, stirring constantly until smooth. Add marshmallows; cook until marshmallows are melted and mixture is smooth, stirring frequently. Stir in liqueur. Cover; refrigerate 40 to 60 minutes or until thickened but not set. Fold in whipped cream. In parfait glasses or dessert dishes, layer pudding and raspberries. Refrigerate at least 2 hours before serving.
7 (½-cup) servings.

MICROWAVE DIRECTIONS:
In 2-quart microwave-safe casserole, microwave chocolate on HIGH for 1½ to 2½ minutes or until melted, stirring once halfway through cooking. Stir in milk until well blended. Add marshmallows. Microwave on HIGH for 2 to 4 minutes or until marshmallows are melted, stirring after every minute. (Marshmallows puff up and do not appear melted. Stir to melt since added cooking can toughen them.) With wire whisk, beat mixture until smooth. Stir in liqueur. Cover; refrigerate 40 to 60 minutes or until thickened but not set. Fold in whipped cream. Continue as directed above.

NUTRIENTS PER 1/7 OF RECIPE

Calories	320	Sodium	35mg
Fat	15g	Potassium	95mg
Cholesterol	50mg		

CARAMEL-TOPPED CHOCOLATE FLAN

CARAMEL
⅓ cup sugar
⅛ teaspoon cream of tartar
2 tablespoons water

FLAN
2 tablespoons sugar
3 ounces sweet cooking chocolate, chopped
1⅓ cups half-and-half
3 eggs
½ teaspoon vanilla
Whipped cream, if desired
Fresh fruit, if desired

In small heavy saucepan, combine all caramel ingredients; blend well. Cook over medium heat until mixture comes to a boil, stirring constantly. Let boil without stirring until mixture begins to caramelize, about 10 to 12 minutes. If mixture darkens in one spot, swirl pan gently. Stir until mixture is a medium caramel color. Immediately pour caramel into bottom of six 6-ounce custard cups; set aside.

Heat oven to 325°F. In small saucepan, combine 2 tablespoons sugar, chocolate and half-and-half. Cook over low heat, stirring constantly until smooth. Remove from heat. In small bowl, combine eggs and vanilla; beat until light and lemon-colored. Gradually add chocolate mixture; blend well.

Carefully pour egg mixture over caramel in custard cups. Place cups in 13 × 9-inch pan. Pour very hot water into pan to within ½ inch of tops of custard cups. Bake at 325°F. for 50 minutes or until knife inserted in center comes out clean. Cool slightly. To serve, unmold onto individual dessert plates. Garnish with whipped cream and fresh fruit. Serve warm or cold. Store in refrigerator. **6 servings.**

NUTRIENTS PER 1/6 OF RECIPE

Calories	300	Sodium	65mg
Fat	17g	Potassium	230mg
Cholesterol	170mg		

Caramel-Topped Chocolate Flan

When this dessert is unmolded, the caramel sauce runs down the sides of the custard. It's wonderful warm or cold.

WHITE CHOCOLATE MOUSSE WITH RASPBERRY

White Chocolate Mousse with Raspberry

Our taste panel enthusiastically put its stamp of approval on this recipe. This refreshing white chocolate mousse is served in a pool of luscious raspberry sauce. Both can be made early in the day for relaxed assembly just before serving.

Creamy Chocolate Mousse

Making sure the chocolate is completely melted is the trick to this elegant, incredibly delicious mousse.

SAUCE
- 2 (10-ounce) packages frozen raspberries with syrup, thawed
- ¼ cup sugar
- 2 tablespoons frozen orange juice concentrate

MOUSSE
- 2 (6-ounce) packages white baking bar, cut into pieces
- 4 cups whipping cream
- 2 teaspoons vanilla

GLAZE
- ½ cup milk chocolate chips
- 1 teaspoon oil

In blender container or food processor bowl with metal blade, combine all sauce ingredients; process until smooth. Strain through fine sieve to remove seeds. Refrigerate.

In medium saucepan over low heat, melt white baking bar with whipping cream, stirring constantly until smooth. Stir in vanilla. Pour into large bowl; cover with plastic wrap. Refrigerate 2 to 3 hours or until mixture is very cold and thickened, stirring occasionally. Using mixer, beat mousse at high speed until stiff peaks form.

In small saucepan over very low heat, melt chocolate chips with oil, stirring constantly until smooth. To serve, place 2 tablespoonfuls sauce on individual dessert plates. Spoon scant ½ cup mousse in center of each plate. Drizzle glaze over mousse and sauce. Garnish as desired. **10 servings.**

NUTRIENTS PER 1/10 OF RECIPE

Calories	660	Sodium	75mg
Fat	49g	Potassium	300mg
Cholesterol	140mg		

CREAMY CHOCOLATE MOUSSE

- 2 cups whipping cream
- 6 ounces sweet cooking chocolate, chopped
- 1 teaspoon vanilla

In medium saucepan, combine whipping cream and chocolate. Using wire whisk, cook over medium heat, stirring constantly until mixture almost comes to a boil. (Chocolate must be melted.) Stir in vanilla. Pour into large bowl; cover with plastic wrap. Refrigerate 4 hours or until very cold. Using mixer, beat whipping cream mixture at high speed until soft peaks form. Spoon into individual dessert dishes. Refrigerate until serving time. Store in refrigerator. **6 servings.**

NUTRIENTS PER 1/6 OF RECIPE

Calories	440	Sodium	40mg
Fat	39g	Potassium	135mg
Cholesterol	109mg		

CHOCOLATE MOUSSE DE MENTHE

- 3-ounce package cream cheese
- ¼ cup semi-sweet chocolate chips
- 1 tablespoon white crème de menthe
- 1 cup whipping cream
- ¼ cup powdered sugar
- Marbled Chocolate Curls, if desired (See Index)

MICROWAVE DIRECTIONS:

In 2-cup microwave-safe measuring cup, combine cream cheese and chocolate chips. Microwave on HIGH for 30 to 40 seconds or until cream cheese and chocolate chips are softened; stir to blend. Add crème de menthe; beat well.

In small bowl, beat whipping cream and powdered sugar until stiff peaks form. Fold in chocolate mixture. Spoon into individual dessert dishes. Garnish with Marbled Chocolate Curls. Serve immediately. **4 (½-cup) servings.**

NUTRIENTS PER 1/4 OF RECIPE

Calories	420	Sodium	90mg
Fat	36g	Potassium	125mg
Cholesterol	110mg		

Chocolate Heart; White Chocolate Piping, page 128

CHOCOLATE HEART

CHOCOLATE CREAM
> 4 ounces (4 squares) semi-sweet chocolate, chopped
> 2 (8-ounce) packages cream cheese, softened
> 2 cups whipping cream
> 2 cups powdered sugar
> 1 tablespoon cherry-flavored liqueur

SAUCE
> 10-ounce package frozen strawberries with syrup, thawed
> 3 tablespoons powdered sugar
> 1 tablespoon cherry-flavored liqueur
> Fresh strawberries, sliced
> **White Chocolate Piping (See Index)**

Line 8-cup heart-shaped or other decorative mold with 2 layers of dampened cheesecloth, extending 2 inches beyond mold. In small saucepan over low heat, melt chocolate, stirring constantly until smooth. Cool. In large bowl, beat cream cheese until fluffy. Gradually add ½ cup of the whipping cream; beat until smooth. Blend in 2 cups powdered sugar, 1 tablespoon liqueur and cooled chocolate; blend well. In small bowl, beat remaining 1½ cups whipping cream until soft peaks form. Fold whipped cream into chocolate mixture. Spoon into cheesecloth-lined mold. Fold extended cheesecloth over top of chocolate mixture. Refrigerate overnight.

In blender container or food processor bowl with metal blade, puree strawberries. Strain through fine sieve to remove seeds. Stir in 3 tablespoons powdered sugar and 1 tablespoon liqueur.

To serve, pull back cheesecloth; invert onto serving plate. Remove cheesecloth. Arrange sliced strawberries on mold. Garnish with White Chocolate Piping. Serve with sauce. Store in refrigerator. **12 to 16 servings.**

COOK'S NOTE
Softening Cream Cheese

Cream cheese can be softened in the microwave. Remove the foil wrapper from an 8-ounce package. Place the cream cheese in a microwave-safe container and microwave it on HIGH for 30 to 45 seconds.

NUTRIENTS PER 1/16 OF RECIPE

Calories	330	Sodium	95mg
Fat	24g	Potassium	110mg
Cholesterol	70mg		

Grasshopper Cheesecake

GRASSHOPPER CHEESECAKE

Grasshopper Cheesecake

This layered cheesecake captures the flavors of a popular after-dinner drink. If white creme de menthe is used and/ or a more intense green color is desired, add a few drops of green food coloring.

CRUST
1¾ cups (35 wafers) crushed chocolate cookie wafers
¼ cup margarine or butter, melted

FILLING
4 eggs
3 (8-ounce) packages cream cheese, softened
1 cup sugar
2 cups dairy sour cream
3 ounces (3 squares) semi-sweet chocolate, melted
¼ cup crème de cacao
¼ cup green creme de menthe

TOPPING
3 ounces (3 squares) semi-sweet chocolate, melted
½ cup dairy sour cream

Heat oven to 325°F. In medium bowl, combine crust ingredients; blend well. Press evenly in bottom and 2 inches up sides of ungreased 10-inch springform pan.

In large bowl, beat eggs until well blended. Add cream cheese and sugar; beat until smooth. Add 2 cups sour cream; blend well. Divide mixture in half. Stir 3 ounces melted chocolate and crème de cacao into half of mixture. Pour into crust-lined pan. Stir creme de menthe into remaining half of mixture. Carefully spoon over chocolate mixture. Bake at 325°F. for 65 to 80 minutes or until center is set. (To minimize cracking, place shallow pan half full of hot water on lower oven rack during baking.) Cool in pan completely.

In small bowl, combine 3 ounces melted chocolate and ½ cup sour cream. Spread over top of cooled cheesecake. Using frosting comb or fork, make spiral design on top of cheesecake. Refrigerate several hours or overnight. Just before serving, carefully run knife around sides of pan to loosen. Remove sides of pan. Store in refrigerator. **16 servings.**

NUTRIENTS PER 1/16 OF RECIPE
Calories	470	Sodium	220mg
Fat	33g	Potassium	180mg
Cholesterol	138mg		

DOUBLE CHOCOLATE CHEESECAKE

No-stick cooking spray
2 tablespoons graham cracker crumbs
1 envelope unflavored gelatin
¼ cup water
2 cups skim or lowfat milk
2 (8-ounce) packages Neufchâtel cheese, softened
½ cup powdered sugar
1 teaspoon vanilla
3½-ounce package instant chocolate fudge pudding and pie filling mix
1½ ounces (1½ squares) white baking bar, chopped
½ ounce (½ square) white baking bar, grated

Spray bottom only of 8-inch springform pan with cooking spray. Sprinkle graham cracker crumbs over bottom; set aside. In small saucepan, combine gelatin and water; let stand 1 minute. Stir over low heat until gelatin is dissolved.

In food processor bowl with metal blade or blender container, combine milk and cheese; process until smooth. With machine running, gradually add gelatin mixture, powdered sugar, vanilla and pudding mix; process until smooth. Stir in chopped white baking bar. Pour into crumb-lined pan. Sprinkle grated white baking bar over cheesecake. Refrigerate 8 hours or until set. Just before serving, carefully run knife around sides of pan to loosen. Remove sides of pan. Store in refrigerator. **12 servings.**

NUTRIENTS PER 1/12 OF RECIPE

Calories	190	Sodium	220mg
Fat	11g	Potassium	135mg
Cholesterol	30mg		

CHOCOLATE CHIP CHEESECAKE

CRUST
2 cups (24 cookies) crushed creme-filled chocolate sandwich cookies
2 tablespoons margarine or butter, melted

FILLING
3 eggs
2 (8-ounce) packages cream cheese, softened
¾ cup sugar
1 teaspoon vanilla
½ cup whipping cream
1 cup miniature semi-sweet chocolate chips

GLAZE
¼ cup miniature semi-sweet chocolate chips
1 teaspoon shortening

Heat oven to 325°F. In medium bowl, combine crust ingredients; blend well. Press evenly in bottom and 1 inch up sides of ungreased 10-inch springform pan.

In large bowl, beat eggs until well blended. Add cream cheese, sugar and vanilla; beat until smooth. Add whipping cream; blend well. Stir in 1 cup chocolate chips. Pour into crust-lined pan. Bake at 325°F. for 60 to 75 minutes or until center is set. (To minimize cracking, place shallow pan half full of hot water on lower oven rack during baking.) Cool in pan completely.

In small saucepan over low heat, melt ¼ cup chocolate chips and shortening, stirring constantly until smooth. Drizzle over cooled cheesecake. Refrigerate several hours or overnight. Just before serving, carefully run knife around sides of pan to loosen. Remove sides of pan. Store in refrigerator. **12 servings.**

NUTRIENTS PER 1/12 OF RECIPE

Calories	450	Sodium	240mg
Fat	31g	Potassium	135mg
Cholesterol	130mg		

Double Chocolate Cheesecake

So velvety smooth and creamy, this no-bake chocolate cheesecake is flecked with white chocolate chunks. Only 190 calories per serving is unbelievable!

Chocolate Chip Cheesecake

This is a traditional cheesecake baked in a chocolate cookie crumb crust. Drizzle the chocolate glaze in a fancy design for a special finishing touch.

Chocolate Orange Cheesecake

CHOCOLATE ORANGE CHEESECAKE

⅓ cup graham cracker crumbs
4 (8-ounce) packages cream cheese, softened
1⅓ cups sugar
4 eggs
2 tablespoons orange-flavored liqueur or orange juice
1 teaspoon grated orange peel
3 ounces (3 squares) semi-sweet chocolate, melted

Heat oven to 325°F. Lightly grease 9-inch springform pan. Sprinkle with graham cracker crumbs over bottom and sides of greased pan. In large bowl, beat cream cheese until light and fluffy. Gradually add sugar; beat well. Add eggs 1 at a time, beating well after each addition. Add liqueur and orange peel. Beat 2 minutes at medium speed, scraping sides of bowl occasionally.

In small bowl, reserve 1½ cups of cream cheese mixture. Pour remaining mixture into greased and crumb-lined pan. Slowly blend melted chocolate into reserved cream cheese mixture. Drop spoonfuls of chocolate mixture onto cream cheese mixture in pan. To marble, pull knife through layers in wide curves.* Bake at 325°F. for 1 hour or until set. (To minimize cracking, place shallow pan half full of hot water on lower oven rack during baking.) Cool in pan completely. Refrigerate several hours or overnight. Top may crack slightly during cooling. Just before serving, carefully run knife around sides of pan to loosen. Remove sides of pan. Store in refrigerator. **16 servings.**

TIP: *To form heart design in top of cheesecake, spoon chocolate mixture by teaspoonfuls onto cream cheese mixture in pan, forming 9 drops around outer edge and 5 drops in ring in center. Continue to spoon chocolate mixture onto drops using all of chocolate mixture. Starting in center of 1 outer drop, run knife through centers of outer drops. Run knife through centers of inner ring of drops, forming 2 separate rings of connected hearts.

NUTRIENTS PER 1/16 OF RECIPE

Calories	330	Sodium	200mg
Fat	23g	Potassium	110mg
Cholesterol	130mg		

CHOCOLATE CHEESECAKE

CRUST
1¾ cups (35 wafers) crushed chocolate cookie wafers
6 tablespoons margarine or butter, melted

FILLING
2 (8-ounce) packages cream cheese, softened
⅔ cup sugar
3 eggs
12-ounce package (2 cups) semi-sweet chocolate chips, melted
1 cup whipping cream
2 tablespoons margarine or butter, melted
1 teaspoon vanilla

Heat oven to 325°F. In medium bowl, combine crust ingredients; blend well. Reserve 1 tablespoonful crumb mixture for garnish. Press remaining crumb mixture evenly in bottom and 2 inches up sides of ungreased 10-inch springform pan. Refrigerate.

In large bowl, combine cream cheese and sugar; beat until light and fluffy. Add eggs 1 at a time, beating well after each addition. Add melted chocolate; beat well. Add whipping cream, 2 tablespoons margarine and vanilla; beat until smooth. Pour into crust-lined pan. Bake at 325°F. for 55 to 65 minutes or until edges are set. Center of cheesecake will be soft. (To minimize cracking, place shallow pan half full of hot water on lower oven rack during baking.) Cool in pan 5 minutes; carefully run knife around sides of pan to loosen. Remove sides of pan. Cool completely. Garnish with reserved crumbs. Refrigerate several hours or overnight. Store in refrigerator. **16 servings.**

NUTRIENTS PER 1/16 OF RECIPE

Calories	440	Sodium	190mg
Fat	32g	Potassium	150mg
Cholesterol	110mg		

COOK'S NOTE
Baking Cheesecakes

A pan of hot water on the oven rack below a cheesecake during baking will minimize cracking on the surface.

CREAMY CHOCOLATE LACE CHEESECAKE

CRUST
1½ cups (30 wafers) crushed chocolate cookie wafers
½ cup finely chopped almonds
¼ cup margarine or butter, melted

FILLING
2 (8-ounce) packages cream cheese, softened
⅔ cup sugar
3 eggs
12-ounce package (2 cups) semi-sweet chocolate chips, melted, cooled
1 cup whipping cream
2 tablespoons margarine or butter, melted
1 teaspoon vanilla

TOPPING
1 cup dairy sour cream
1½ teaspoons vanilla
1 teaspoon sugar
½ ounce (½ square) unsweetened chocolate, melted

Heat oven to 325°F. Butter 9-inch springform pan. In large bowl, combine all crust ingredients; blend well. Press evenly in bottom and up sides of buttered pan. Refrigerate.

In large bowl, combine cream cheese and ⅔ cup sugar; beat until smooth. Add eggs 1 at a time, beating well after each addition. Add melted chocolate chips; beat well. Add whipping cream, 2 tablespoons margarine and 1 teaspoon vanilla; beat until smooth. Pour into crust-lined pan. Bake at 325°F. for 55 to 65 minutes or until edges are set. Center of cheesecake will be soft. (To minimize cracking, place shallow pan half full of hot water on lower oven rack during baking.) Cool in pan 5 minutes; carefully run knife around sides of pan to loosen. Remove sides of pan. Cool completely.

In small bowl, combine sour cream, 1½ teaspoons vanilla and 1 teaspoon sugar; blend until smooth. Spread over cooled cheesecake. Drizzle top of cheesecake with ½ ounce melted chocolate in lace pattern. Refrigerate several hours or overnight. Garnish as desired. Store in refrigerator. **16 servings.**

NUTRIENTS PER 1/16 OF RECIPE

Calories	470	Sodium	180mg
Fat	36g	Potassium	200mg
Cholesterol	110mg		

Creme de Menthe Cheesecake Squares

When cheesecake is desired for a large group, serve this rich and creamy dessert. Serve each piece garnished with a mint leaf and Chocolate Curl (See Index).

COOK'S NOTE
Removing Cheesecakes from Pans

Use a sharp knife to loosen a cheesecake from the pan. Run the knife carefully around the edge.

CREME DE MENTHE CHEESECAKE SQUARES

CRUST
1¾ cups (35 wafers) crushed chocolate cookie wafers
½ cup margarine or butter, melted

FILLING
2 (8-ounce) packages cream cheese, softened
½ cup dairy sour cream
4 eggs
⅔ cup sugar
½ cup creme de menthe syrup
¼ teaspoon mint extract

TOPPING
4 ounces (4 squares) semi-sweet chocolate, cut into pieces
½ cup dairy sour cream

Heat oven to 350°F. In medium bowl, combine crust ingredients; blend well. Press evenly in bottom and 1 inch up sides of ungreased 13 × 9-inch pan. Freeze crust while preparing filling.

In large bowl, combine all filling ingredients. Beat on low speed until smooth. Pour into crust-lined pan. Bake at 350°F. for 30 to 35 minutes or until knife inserted in center comes out clean. Cool on wire rack.

In small saucepan over low heat, melt chocolate, stirring constantly until smooth. Cool 5 minutes. Using wire whisk, beat in sour cream. Spread over warm cheesecake. Refrigerate 3 hours or until firm. Cut into squares. Store in refrigerator. **20 servings.**

NUTRIENTS PER 1/20 OF RECIPE

Calories	300	Sodium	160mg
Fat	20g	Potassium	95mg
Cholesterol	90mg		

Chocolate Lover's Cheesecake

CHOCOLATE LOVER'S CHEESECAKE

CRUST
- 1¾ cups (35 wafers) crushed chocolate cookie wafers
- ¼ cup sugar
- ⅓ cup margarine or butter, melted

FILLING
- 3 (8-ounce) packages cream cheese, softened
- 1 cup sugar
- 3 tablespoons flour
- 4-ounce bar sweet cooking chocolate, melted, cooled
- 3 eggs
- 2 tablespoons half-and-half
- 2 teaspoons vanilla

TOPPING
- ½ cup dairy sour cream
- ½ teaspoon vanilla

Heat oven to 400°F. In small bowl, combine all crust ingredients; blend well. Press evenly in bottom and 2 inches up sides of ungreased 9-inch springform pan.

In large bowl, combine cream cheese, 1 cup sugar, flour and chocolate; beat until light and fluffy. Add eggs 1 at a time, beating well after each addition. Blend in half-and-half and 2 teaspoons vanilla. Pour into crust-lined pan. Bake at 400°F. for 10 minutes. Reduce oven temperature to 300°F. Bake an additional 55 to 65 minutes or until filling is set. (To minimize cracking, place shallow pan half full of hot water on lower oven rack during baking.) Cool in pan 10 minutes; carefully run knife around sides of pan to loosen.

In small bowl, combine topping ingredients; blend until smooth. Spread over slightly cooled cheesecake. Refrigerate until serving time. Just before serving, remove sides of pan. Garnish as desired. Store in refrigerator. **16 servings.**

NUTRIENTS PER 1/16 OF RECIPE

Calories	390	Sodium	210mg
Fat	26g	Potassium	120mg
Cholesterol	108mg		

Pictured clockwise from top left: Cappuccino Fudge, page 103; Chocolate Fudge, page 102; Peppermint Candy Fudge, page 103

Fudges & Candies

Here's proof that making chocolate candy snacks is fun! It wasn't always so, but the new techniques used in these recipes enable novice cooks as well as candy pros to enjoy success every time.

The microwave oven is used extensively in this chapter. Microwaving is a fast and easy way to make a wide variety of candy, such as Microwave Meltaway Fudge, Marble Peanut Bark or Cashew Clusters. It cuts down on the need for careful, constant attention to a hot mixture that could easily scorch. And it dramatically reduces total preparation time, which means that you can enjoy the results of your effort sooner!

Stove-top cooking directions are also included. And you'll find recipes that evoke fond memories of traditional candies with interesting new twists. There's Pat-in-Pan Chocolate Fudge, Cappuccino Fudge and the lighter rendition, White Fudge. If you're the adventurous type, try Macadamia Orange Fudge — an intensely orange and chocolate confection that's nut-crunchy and incredibly good.

Candymaking is something the whole family can share and enjoy, or it can be a delightful party activity. Organize one team to make Dipped Peppermint Creams and Snapping Turtles. Assign others to production of Choco-Caramel Nut Puddles. Decorated with dried fruits and nuts, these easy-to-make sweets look as if they came from the best candy shop.

But candy can be more than candy, and that's when it becomes dessert. What could be more enchanting than after-dinner coffee served with Cherry Nougat Fudge Slices or sinfully rich and delicious Chocolate Caramel Diamonds.

Now that candy can be made so quickly and easily, a chocolate craving can be satisfied in moments. Can you wait that long?

CHOCOLATE FUDGE

2½ cups sugar
½ cup margarine or butter
5-ounce can (about ½ cup) evaporated milk
7-ounce jar (2 cups) marshmallow creme
12-ounce package (2 cups) semi-sweet chocolate chips
¾ cup chopped walnuts
1 teaspoon vanilla

Line 9-inch square or 13 × 9-inch pan with foil so that foil extends over sides of pan; butter foil. In large saucepan, combine sugar, margarine and milk. Bring to a boil over medium heat, stirring constantly. Boil 5 minutes, stirring constantly. Remove from heat. Add marshmallow creme and chocolate chips; blend until smooth. Stir in walnuts and vanilla. Pour into buttered foil-lined pan. Cool to room temperature. Score fudge into 36 or 48 squares. Refrigerate until firm. Remove fudge from pan by lifting foil; remove foil from sides of fudge. Using large knife, cut through scored lines. Store in refrigerator.
About 3 pounds (36 or 48 squares).

MICROWAVE DIRECTIONS:

Prepare pan as directed above. In 2-quart microwave-safe bowl, combine sugar, margarine and evaporated milk. Microwave on HIGH for 6 to 8 minutes or until mixture comes to a rolling boil, stirring twice during cooking. Add marshmallow creme and chocolate chips; blend until smooth. Stir in walnuts and vanilla. Continue as directed above.

⌘

COOK'S NOTE
Making Fudge

Our fudges are less temperamental than the old-timers, but they taste just as flavorful and have the same satiny texture. They mail beautifully and store well when tightly covered in the refrigerator.

Butterscotch Fudge: Prepare fudge as directed in recipe, substituting 12-ounce package butterscotch chips for chocolate chips and pecans for walnuts.

Confetti Fudge: Prepare fudge as directed in recipe, substituting 2 cups candy-coated chocolate pieces for walnuts. Stir 1½ cups of the chocolate pieces into fudge with vanilla. Pour into buttered, foil-lined pan. Sprinkle remaining ½ cup chocolate pieces over top; press lightly into warm fudge. Cool to room temperature. Do not refrigerate before cutting. Score and cut fudge as directed in recipe. Store in refrigerator. Let stand at room temperature before serving.

Rocky Road Fudge: Prepare fudge as directed in recipe. Stir in 2 cups miniature marshmallows after walnuts and vanilla. (Marshmallows should not melt completely.) Quickly spread in buttered foil-lined pan. Continue as directed in recipe.

Turtle Fudge: Prepare fudge as directed in recipe, substituting cashews for walnuts. Stir in 24 unwrapped, quartered caramels with cashews and vanilla. Cool to room temperature. Do not refrigerate before cutting. Score and cut fudge as directed in recipe. Store in refrigerator. Let stand at room temperature before serving.

NUTRIENTS PER 1 SQUARE CHOCOLATE FUDGE

Calories	130	Sodium	30mg
Fat	6g	Potassium	45mg
Cholesterol	0mg		

WHITE FUDGE

2½ cups sugar
½ cup margarine or butter
5-ounce can (about ½ cup) evaporated milk
7-ounce jar (2 cups) marshmallow creme
8 ounces vanilla-flavored candy coating, coarsely chopped
¾ cup chopped walnuts
1 teaspoon vanilla

Line 9-inch square or 13 × 9-inch pan with foil so that foil extends over sides of pan; butter foil. In large saucepan, combine sugar, margarine and milk. Bring to a boil over medium heat, stirring constantly. Boil 5 minutes, stirring constantly. Remove from heat. Add marshmallow creme and candy coating; blend until smooth. Stir in walnuts and vanilla. Pour into buttered foil-lined pan. Cool to room temperature. Score fudge into 36 or 48 squares. Refrigerate until firm. Remove fudge from pan by lifting foil; remove foil from sides of fudge. Using large knife, cut through scored lines. Store in refrigerator.

About 2½ pounds (36 or 48 squares).

Christmas Fudge: Prepare fudge as directed in recipe, substituting ½ cup chopped almonds for walnuts and ¼ teaspoon almond extract for vanilla. Stir in ½ cup chopped dates and ½ cup chopped red candied cherries with almonds and almond extract.

Peanut Butter Fudge: Prepare fudge as directed in recipe, decreasing candy coating to 6 ounces. Add ½ cup peanut butter with marshmallow creme and candy coating. Substitute ¾ cup chopped dry roasted peanuts for walnuts.

Peppermint Candy Fudge: Prepare fudge as directed in recipe, substituting ½ cup finely crushed peppermint candies for walnuts. Omit vanilla. Add desired amount of red food coloring with crushed candies.

NUTRIENTS PER 1 SQUARE WHITE FUDGE

Calories	130	Sodium	40mg
Fat	5g	Potassium	45mg
Cholesterol	1mg		

CAPPUCCINO FUDGE

1 tablespoon boiling water
1 tablespoon instant coffee granules or crystals
1 teaspoon cinnamon
2½ cups sugar
½ cup margarine or butter
5-ounce can (about ½ cup) evaporated milk
7-ounce jar (2 cups) marshmallow creme
12 ounce package (2 cups) semi sweet chocolate chips
1 teaspoon vanilla

Line 9-inch square or 13 × 9-inch pan with foil so that foil extends over sides of pan; butter foil. In small bowl, combine boiling water, instant coffee and cinnamon; set aside. In large saucepan, combine sugar, margarine and evaporated milk. Bring to a boil over medium heat, stirring constantly. Boil 5 minutes, stirring constantly. Remove from heat. Add marshmallow creme, chocolate chips, vanilla and coffee-cinnamon mixture; blend until smooth. Pour into buttered foil-lined pan. Cool to room temperature. Score fudge into 36 or 48 squares. Garnish as desired. Refrigerate until firm. Remove fudge from pan by lifting foil; remove foil from sides of fudge. Using large knife, cut through scored lines. Store in refrigerator.

About 3 pounds (36 or 48 squares).

MICROWAVE DIRECTIONS:
Prepare pan as directed above. In small bowl, combine boiling water, instant coffee and cinnamon; set aside. In 2-quart microwave-safe bowl, combine sugar, margarine and evaporated milk. Microwave on HIGH for 6 to 8 minutes or until mixture comes to a rolling boil, stirring twice during cooking. Add marshmallow creme, chocolate chips, vanilla and coffee-cinnamon mixture; blend until smooth. Continue as directed above.

NUTRIENTS PER 1 SQUARE

Calories	110	Sodium	30mg
Fat	4g	Potassium	40mg
Cholesterol	0mg		

Cherry Nougat Fudge Slices

CHERRY NOUGAT FUDGE SLICES

NOUGAT
- 1 envelope unflavored gelatin
- 3 tablespoons water
- ¼ cup sugar
- ⅓ cup light corn syrup
- 1 teaspoon vanilla
- 2 to 2½ cups powdered sugar
- ½ cup chopped red candied cherries

CARAMEL
- 14-ounce package fudge-flavored caramels, unwrapped
- 2 tablespoons corn syrup
- 1 cup chopped toasted almonds*

MICROWAVE DIRECTIONS:
Generously butter 8 × 4-inch rectangle on each of 3 sheets of waxed paper. In small microwave-safe bowl, combine gelatin and water; let stand 5 minutes. Stir in sugar and ⅓ cup corn syrup. Microwave on HIGH for 2 to 2½ minutes or until mixture comes to a boil, stirring once halfway through cooking. Cool 5 minutes. Add vanilla. Beat on high speed until soft peaks form, 5 to 8 minutes. Stir in 1 cup of the powdered sugar and cherries. Gradually stir in ½ to ¾ cup powdered sugar. On surface sprinkled lightly with powdered sugar, knead in an additional ½ to ¾ cup powdered sugar until mixture is easy to handle and no longer sticky. Divide mixture into thirds. Shape each third into 8-inch log; set aside.

Place ⅓ of the caramels in small microwave-safe bowl. Microwave on HIGH for 20 to 40 seconds or until soft, stirring once halfway through cooking. *Do not melt.* On buttered waxed paper, press softened caramels into 8 × 4-inch rectangle. Place nougat log on center of rectangle; wrap caramel around log. Repeat with remaining nougat logs and caramels.

Brush logs with 2 tablespoons corn syrup. Roll logs in almonds. Wrap in waxed paper; refrigerate. To serve, cut crosswise into ½-inch slices. (Dip knife into hot water if necessary to minimize sticking.) Store candies between sheets of waxed paper in loosely covered container in cool, dry place.
4 dozen candies.

TIP: *To toast 1 cup almonds, spread in thin layer in microwave-safe pie pan. Microwave on HIGH for 5 to 7 minutes or until light golden brown, stirring once every minute.

NUTRIENTS PER 1 CANDY

Calories	90	Sodium	20mg
Fat	2g	Potassium	40mg
Cholesterol	0mg		

PAT-IN-PAN CHOCOLATE FUDGE

- ½ cup margarine or butter
- 8-ounce package cream cheese
- 3 ounces (3 squares) unsweetened chocolate
- 6 cups powdered sugar

Line 13 × 9-inch pan with foil so that foil extends over sides of pan. In large saucepan, combine margarine, cream cheese and chocolate. Cook over low heat until mixture is just melted and smooth, stirring constantly. Remove from heat. Add powdered sugar 1 cup at a time, mixing well after each addition. Knead if necessary. Press mixture evenly into foil-lined pan. Refrigerate until firm. Remove fudge from pan by lifting foil; remove foil from sides of fudge. Cut into squares or desired shapes. Decorate as desired. Store in refrigerator.
About 2½ pounds.

NUTRIENTS PER 1 OUNCE

Calories	110	Sodium	45mg
Fat	5g	Potassium	25mg
Cholesterol	6mg		

COOK'S NOTE
Making Candy in a Microwave

When making candy in the microwave, avoid boilovers by using a container two to three times greater than the volume being cooked. Do not cover the container. An uncovered container allows unwanted moisture to escape and simplifies stirring.

MACADAMIA ORANGE FUDGE

Macadamia Orange Fudge

This fudge has a wonderfully intense orange flavor with the crunchy texture of macadamia nuts. Garnish the squares with small pieces of grated orange peel.

Microwave Meltaway Fudge

Many imitation chocolate products exist in today's market and discerning shoppers compare their flavor, performance, nutrition and value with the "real thing." For best flavor and quality, we recommend real chocolate chips for this creamy microwave fudge.

2½ cups sugar
½ cup margarine or butter
5-ounce can (about ½ cup) evaporated milk
7-ounce jar (2 cups) marshmallow creme
12-ounce package (2 cups) semi-sweet chocolate chips
3.5-ounce jar macadamia nuts, chopped
2 tablespoons orange-flavored liqueur or orange juice
1 tablespoon finely grated orange peel

Line a 13 × 9-inch pan with foil so that foil extends over sides of pan; lightly butter foil. In large saucepan, combine sugar, margarine and evaporated milk. Bring to a boil over medium heat, stirring constantly. Boil 5 minutes, stirring constantly. Remove from heat. Add marshmallow creme and chocolate chips; blend until smooth. Stir in macadamia nuts, liqueur and orange peel. Pour into buttered, foil-lined pan. Cool to room temperature. Score fudge into 36 or 48 squares. Refrigerate until firm. Remove fudge from pan by lifting foil; remove foil from sides of fudge. Using large knife, cut through scored lines. Store in refrigerator.

3 pounds (36 or 48 squares).

MICROWAVE DIRECTIONS:

Prepare pan as directed above. In 2-quart microwave-safe bowl, combine sugar, margarine and evaporated milk. Microwave on HIGH for 6 to 8 minutes or until mixture comes to a rolling boil, stirring twice during cooking. Add marshmallow creme and chocolate chips; blend until smooth. Continue as directed above.

NUTRIENTS PER 1 SQUARE

Calories	130	Sodium	30mg
Fat	6g	Potassium	45mg
Cholesterol	0mg		

MICROWAVE MELTAWAY FUDGE

12-ounce package (2 cups) semi-sweet chocolate chips
14-ounce can sweetened condensed milk (not evaporated)
1 teaspoon vanilla

MICROWAVE DIRECTIONS:

Line 8-inch square pan with foil so foil extends over sides of pan; butter foil. In 2½-quart microwave-safe bowl or 8-cup microwave-safe measuring cup, combine chocolate chips and sweetened condensed milk. Microwave on HIGH for 1½ to 1¾ minutes or until chocolate is melted, stirring once halfway through cooking. Stir until smooth. Add vanilla; blend well. Pour into buttered foil-lined pan. Refrigerate until firm.

Remove fudge from pan by lifting foil; remove foil from sides of fudge. Using large knife, cut into squares. Store in covered container in refrigerator.

1 pound 9 ounces.

CONVENTIONAL DIRECTIONS:

Prepare pan as directed above. In medium saucepan over low heat, melt chocolate chips with sweetened condensed milk, stirring constantly until smooth. Continue as directed above.

Black Forest Fudge: Prepare fudge as directed in recipe, substituting ¼ teaspoon almond extract for vanilla. Stir ⅔ cup chopped red candied cherries, ½ cup chopped almonds and ½ cup miniature marshmallows into melted chocolate mixture with almond extract.

Rocky Road Fudge: Prepare fudge as directed in recipe. Stir 1 cup miniature marshmallows and ½ cup chopped nuts into melted chocolate with vanilla.

NUTRIENTS PER 1 OUNCE

Calories	150	Sodium	25mg
Fat	7g	Potassium	125mg
Cholesterol	6mg		

Dipped Peppermint Creams

DIPPED PEPPERMINT CREAMS

CANDY
- 16 ounces vanilla-flavored candy coating, cut into pieces
- ¼ cup shortening
- ½ cup finely crushed peppermint candy*

COATING
- 4 ounces chocolate-flavored candy coating, cut into pieces
- 1 tablespoon shortening

Line 9 × 5-inch loaf pan with foil. In medium saucepan over low heat, melt vanilla-flavored candy coating and ¼ cup shortening, stirring constantly until smooth. Remove from heat; stir in peppermint candy. Spread in foil-lined pan. Let stand at room temperature until firm. Remove candy from pan by lifting foil; remove foil from sides of candy. Cut into 1-inch squares. Let candy harden completely.

In small saucepan over low heat, melt coating ingredients, stirring constantly until smooth. Set saucepan in hot water to maintain dipping consistency. Dip half of each peppermint candy square into coating; allow excess to drip off. Place coated side up on waxed paper. Garnish as desired. Let stand until set. Store in single layer at room temperature. **32 candies.**

MICROWAVE DIRECTIONS:
Prepare pan as directed above. In medium microwave-safe bowl, combine vanilla-flavored candy coating and ¼ cup shortening. Microwave on MEDIUM for 3 to 5 minutes or until candy coating is melted; stir until smooth. Stir in peppermint candy. Continue as directed above.

To prepare coating, in medium microwave-safe bowl, combine coating ingredients. Microwave on MEDIUM for 2 to 3 minutes or until melted; stir until smooth. Dip and store candies as directed above.

TIP: *To crush peppermint candies, place in plastic bag; secure with twist tie. Using hammer, crush candies.

NUTRIENTS PER 1 CANDY

Calories	130	Sodium	10mg
Fat	9g	Potassium	30mg
Cholesterol	0mg		

Dipped Peppermint Creams

Make your very own dipped chocolates using vanilla and chocolate-flavored candy coating. These candies store best at room temperature.

Pictured top to bottom: Marble Peanut Bark; Choco-Caramel Nut Puddles

CHOCO-CARAMEL NUT PUDDLES

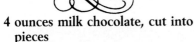

4 ounces milk chocolate, cut into
  pieces
4 ounces chocolate-flavored candy
  coating, cut into pieces
10 caramels, unwrapped
2 teaspoons milk
  Dried quartered apricots
  Pecan halves
  Raisins
  Whole blanched almonds

Line cookie sheets with waxed paper.
Using pencil, draw thirty-six 1½-inch
circles 2 inches apart on waxed paper-
lined cookie sheets. In medium heavy
saucepan over low heat, melt milk
chocolate and candy coating, stirring
constantly until smooth. Spoon and
spread 1 tablespoonful chocolate mixture onto each circle. Refrigerate about
10 minutes or until chocolate is set.

In small saucepan over low heat, melt
caramels with milk, stirring constantly
until smooth. Spoon about ½ teaspoonful caramel mixture onto each chocolate circle, leaving ½ inch chocolate
showing around edge. Decorate with
combinations of dried fruits and nuts;
press down lightly. Refrigerate until
set. Gently remove candies from waxed
paper. Store in single layer in tightly
covered container. **2 dozen candies.**

MICROWAVE DIRECTIONS:
Draw circles as directed above. In medium microwave-safe bowl, combine
milk chocolate and candy coating. Microwave on MEDIUM for 3 to 4 minutes or until melted, stirring once
halfway through cooking. Stir until
smooth. Spoon and spread 1 tablespoonful chocolate mixture onto each
circle on waxed paper-lined cookie
sheets. Refrigerate about 10 minutes or
until chocolate is set. In small microwave-safe bowl, combine caramels and
milk. Microwave on MEDIUM for 2½
to 3 minutes or until melted, stirring
once every minute. Stir until smooth.
Continue as directed above.

NUTRIENTS PER 1 CANDY
Calories	80	Sodium	15mg
Fat	4g	Potassium	55mg
Cholesterol	0mg		

MILK CHOCOLATE PEANUT BUTTER BARK

1 cup milk chocolate chips
1 cup peanut butter chips
½ cup coarsely chopped salted
  peanuts

Line 13 × 9-inch pan with foil. In medium saucepan over low heat, melt
milk chocolate chips and peanut butter
chips, stirring constantly until smooth.
Stir in peanuts. Pour into foil-lined pan;
spread evenly to cover bottom. Refrigerate 1 hour or until set. Remove candy
from pan by lifting foil; remove foil.
Break candy into pieces. Store in refrigerator. **About 1 pound.**

NUTRIENTS PER 1 OUNCE
Calories	150	Sodium	45mg
Fat	9g	Potassium	115mg
Cholesterol	0mg		

MARBLE PEANUT BARK

1 cup milk chocolate chips
1 cup vanilla milk chips or 6
  ounces vanilla-flavored candy
  coating, cut into pieces
½ cup coarsely chopped salted
  peanuts

Line 13 × 9-inch pan with foil. In small
saucepan over low heat, melt milk
chocolate chips, stirring constantly
until smooth. Keep warm. In another
small saucepan over low heat, melt vanilla milk chips, stirring constantly until
smooth. Pour melted milk chocolate
into foil-lined pan; spread evenly to
cover bottom. Sprinkle with peanuts.
Pour melted vanilla milk chips over
milk chocolate. To marble, pull knife
through layers in wide curves. Refrigerate 1 hour or until set. Remove candy
from pan by lifting foil; remove foil.
Break candy into pieces. Store in refrigerator. **14 ounces.**

NUTRIENTS PER 1 OUNCE
Calories	160	Sodium	70mg
Fat	10g	Potassium	130mg
Cholesterol	2mg		

*Choco-Caramel
Nut Puddles*

Topped with dried fruits and
nuts, these easy but elegant
chocolate confections look just
as if they came from your favorite candy shop.

*Marble
Peanut Bark*

White and milk chocolate are
swirled together and sprinkled
with peanuts to make an irresistible bark. Store this candy
in the refrigerator.

Snapping Turtles

SNAPPING TURTLES

6-ounce package (1 cup) semi-
  sweet chocolate chips
½ cup ready-to-spread coconut
  pecan frosting
½ cup salted whole cashews

Line cookie sheet with waxed paper.
Using pencil, draw twelve 1½-inch circles 2 inches apart on waxed paper-
lined cookie sheet. In small saucepan
over low heat, melt chocolate, stirring
constantly until smooth. Spoon and
spread 1 teaspoonful melted chocolate
onto each circle. Reserve remaining
chocolate. Reserve 12 whole cashews.
Split remaining cashews in half lengthwise; save broken pieces. Press wide
ends of 4 cashew halves into chocolate
circle to make feet. Refrigerate 30 minutes or until chocolate is set.

To assemble turtles, place about 1½
teaspoonfuls of frosting in center of
each chocolate circle. Reheat reserved
chocolate. Spoon over frosting to make
turtle shells. Press 1 end of a whole
cashew in each turtle shell to make
head. Press broken piece of cashew in
each turtle shell to make tail. Refrigerate until set. Store in refrigerator.
12 candies.

NUTRIENTS PER 1 CANDY

Calories	150	Sodium	15mg
Fat	10g	Potassium	90mg
Cholesterol	0mg		

CASHEW CLUSTERS

12-ounce package (2 cups) semi-
  sweet chocolate chips
1 ounce (1 square) unsweetened
  chocolate
2 cups cashews

Line cookie sheets with waxed paper.
In large saucepan over low heat, melt
chocolate chips and chocolate, stirring
constantly until smooth. Stir in cashews. Drop candy by teaspoonfuls onto
waxed paper-lined cookie sheets. Refrigerate until set. Store in tightly covered container in refrigerator.
3 dozen candies.

MICROWAVE DIRECTIONS:
Prepare cookie sheets as directed
above. In 1-quart microwave-safe casserole, combine chocolate chips and
chocolate. Microwave on HIGH for 2½
to 3½ minutes or until melted, stirring
once halfway during cooking. Continue
as directed above.

NUTRIENTS PER 1 CANDY

Calories	100	Sodium	0mg
Fat	7g	Potassium	80mg
Cholesterol	0mg		

CHOCOLATE CARAMEL DIAMONDS

1 cup butter
1¼ cups sugar
1 cup firmly packed brown sugar
1 cup light corn syrup
14-ounce can sweetened condensed
  milk (not evaporated)
2 ounces (2 squares) semi-sweet
  chocolate, chopped
2 teaspoons vanilla

Line 9-inch square pan with foil so that
foil extends over sides of pan; butter
foil. In medium-heavy saucepan over
low heat, melt 1 cup butter. Add sugar,
brown sugar and corn syrup. Cook over
medium-low heat until sugar dissolves
and mixture is well blended, stirring
constantly. Stir in sweetened condensed milk. Cook over medium heat,
stirring constantly until mixture
reaches 230°F. on candy thermometer,
about 30 minutes. Stir in chocolate;
cook until mixture reaches soft-ball
stage (240°F.), 15 to 20 minutes. Remove from heat. Stir in vanilla.

Pour into buttered foil-lined pan. Cool.
Refrigerate several hours or until candy
is set. Remove candy from pan by lifting foil; remove foil from sides of
candy. Using large knife, cut into diamond shapes or squares. Store in covered container.
2¾ pounds (about 40 diamond
shapes).

NUTRIENTS PER 1 DIAMOND

Calories	140	Sodium	60mg
Fat	5g	Potassium	60mg
Cholesterol	15mg		

Cashew Clusters

*When melting chocolate, use
utensils that are completely
dry. Melt the chocolate slowly
and over very low heat, stirring
constantly.*

COOK'S NOTE
Candy Thermometer

To remove any guesswork,
some of our recipes use a
candy thermometer. For the
best-quality product, watch
temperatures carefully.

Pictured top to bottom: German Chocolate Streusel Coffee Cake, page 118; Chocolate Almond Crescent Braid, page 115

Breads, Sweet Rolls & Coffee Cakes

milling and baking, and
are skilled in making all
manner of br and sweet rolls. Many have
also professed a passio ny not marry the two," we
said. And so we did, cr ng n of recipes for those who
thought they had expe ced just about every chocolate delight im-
aginable.

Chocolate now gr s the breakfast table in the form of waffles,
scones, pancakes an muffins. We've all enjoyed the pull-apart ring
featuring biscuits r ed in butter and a sugar-cinnamon mixture. A new
version in this ch pter, Chocolate Surprise Biscuit Ring, features biscuit
dough wrappe around milk chocolate candy kisses.

A special eekend breakfast or brunch is a great time to show off
your best b ead-and-chocolate combos. Treat yourself to Quick Chocolate Cara el Rolls, the traditional sticky bun with a chocolate filling.
Or start t e day with Swirled Chocolate Sweet Rolls, so easy to make
with hot oll mix.

From arly morning to midnight, there's often an occasion that is
well sui ed for chocolate breads. Chocolate Rich Crescent Croissants,
Chocol te Peanut Butter Roll-Ups and Chocolate Almond Crescent
Braid a e irresistible treats. These recipes feature refrigerated crescent
dinner oll dough shaped in uniquely attractive ways.

Some imes bread can double as dessert. German Chocolate Streusel
Coffee Cake is such a recipe. Use one warm from the oven and freeze
the oth r for emergency treatment when a chocolate attack occurs
without warning.

There s always something special about hot-from-the-oven treats,
and the ragrance and flavor of chocolate make the experience truly
extraordinary.

QUICK CHOCOLATE CARAMEL ROLLS

TOPPING
½ cup firmly packed brown sugar
¼ cup chopped nuts
½ cup margarine or butter, softened
2 tablespoons corn syrup

ROLLS
3 to 3½ cups all purpose or unbleached flour
¼ cup sugar
1 teaspoon salt
1 package active dry yeast
1 cup water
2 tablespoons margarine or butter
1 egg

FILLING
½ cup semi-sweet chocolate chips
2 tablespoons margarine or butter, softened
¼ cup finely chopped nuts

Grease 13 × 9-inch pan. In small bowl, combine all topping ingredients; blend well. Drop mixture by spoonfuls into greased pan; spread evenly to cover bottom. Set aside.

Lightly spoon flour into measuring cup; level off. In large bowl, combine 1½ cups flour, sugar, salt and yeast; blend well. In small saucepan, heat water and 2 tablespoons margarine until very warm (120 to 130°F.). Add warm liquid and egg to flour mixture. Blend at low speed until moistened; beat 3 minutes at medium speed. By hand, stir in 1½ to 2 cups flour until dough pulls cleanly away from sides of bowl. On floured surface, knead dough 1 minute. Roll dough to 15 × 7-inch rectangle.

In small saucepan over low heat, melt chocolate chips and 2 tablespoons margarine, stirring constantly until smooth. Cool until slightly thickened. Spread over dough; sprinkle with nuts. Starting with 15-inch side, roll up tightly; press edges to seal. Cut into 12 slices; place cut side down over topping in pan. Cover loosely with plastic wrap and cloth towel. Let rise in warm place (80 to 85°F.) until light and doubled in size, 35 to 45 minutes.

Heat oven to 375°F. Uncover dough. Bake 25 to 30 minutes or until golden brown. Cool 1 minute; invert onto serving platter or foil. **12 rolls.**

HIGH ALTITUDE Above 3500 Feet: Bake at 375°F. for 20 to 25 minutes.

NUTRIENTS PER 1 ROLL

Calories	380	Sodium	320mg
Fat	18g	Potassium	140mg
Cholesterol	23mg		

***Buttermilk
Chocolate Bread***

———— ❧ ————

Serve this delicious cocoa-flavored bread with Chocolate Honey Butter (See Index).

BUTTERMILK CHOCOLATE BREAD

1 cup sugar
½ cup margarine or butter, softened
2 eggs
1 cup buttermilk*
1¾ cups all purpose or unbleached flour
½ cup unsweetened cocoa
½ teaspoon baking powder
½ teaspoon baking soda
½ teaspoon salt
⅓ cup chopped nuts

Heat oven to 350°F. Grease bottom only of 8 × 4 or 9 × 5-inch loaf pan. In large bowl, combine sugar and margarine; beat until light and fluffy. Add eggs; blend well. Stir in buttermilk. Lightly spoon flour into measuring cup; level off. Add flour, cocoa, baking powder, baking soda and salt; stir just until dry ingredients are moistened. Stir in nuts. Pour into greased pan. Bake at 350°F. for 55 to 65 minutes or until toothpick inserted in center comes out clean. Cool in pan 15 minutes. Remove from pan; cool completely before slicing. **1 (12-slice) loaf.**

TIP: *To substitute for buttermilk, use 1 tablespoon vinegar or lemon juice plus milk to make 1 cup.

HIGH ALTITUDE—Above 3500 Feet: Increase flour to 1¾ cups plus 1 tablespoon. Bake at 375°F. for 50 to 55 minutes.

NUTRIENTS PER 1 SLICE

Calories	260	Sodium	300mg
Fat	12g	Potassium	105mg
Cholesterol	45mg		

CHOCOLATE ALMOND CRESCENT BRAID

BRAID
>   2 ounces (2 squares) semi-sweet chocolate, melted, cooled
>   ⅓ cup sugar
>   ¼ cup dairy sour cream
>   2 tablespoons chopped toasted almonds*
>   8-ounce can refrigerated crescent dinner rolls

GLAZE
>   ½ cup powdered sugar
>   ¼ teaspoon almond extract
>   3 to 4 teaspoons milk
>   2 tablespoons sliced or slivered toasted almonds*

Heat oven to 350°F. In small bowl, combine chocolate, sugar and sour cream; blend until smooth. Stir in 2 tablespoons chopped almonds. Unroll dough into 2 long rectangles. Place on ungreased cookie sheet with long sides overlapping ½ inch; roll out to form 14×7-inch rectangle. Firmly press edges and perforations to seal. Spread chocolate mixture in 2-inch strip lengthwise down center of dough to within ¼ inch of each end. Make cuts 2 inches apart on long sides of rectangle to within ½ inch of filling. To give braided appearance, fold strips of dough at an angle halfway across filling, alternating sides. Fold ends of braid under to seal.

Bake at 350°F. for 18 to 23 minutes or until golden brown. Cool 5 minutes; remove from cookie sheet. Cool on wire rack. In small bowl, blend powdered sugar, almond extract and enough milk for desired drizzling consistency. Drizzle over warm braid. Sprinkle with 2 tablespoons sliced almonds. Cut into slices. **8 servings.**

TIP: *To toast almonds, spread on cookie sheet; bake at 375°F. for 3 to 5 minutes or until light golden brown, stirring occasionally. Or spread in thin layer in microwave-safe pie pan. Microwave on HIGH for 2 to 4 minutes or until light golden brown, stirring frequently.

NUTRIENTS PER 1/8 OF RECIPE
Calories	240	Sodium	240mg
Fat	12g	Potassium	125mg
Cholesterol	6mg		

CHOCOLATE PEANUT BUTTER ROLL-UPS

>   8-ounce can refrigerated crescent dinner rolls
>   8 teaspoons creamy peanut butter
>   8 teaspoons sugar
>   8 teaspoons miniature semi-sweet chocolate chips
>   Sugar

Heat oven to 375°F. Separate dough into 8 triangles. Spread 1 teaspoon peanut butter on each triangle. Sprinkle each with 1 teaspoon sugar. Place 1 teaspoon chocolate chips on shortest side of each triangle. Roll up, starting at shortest side of triangle and rolling to opposite point. Roll each in sugar. Place point side down on ungreased cookie sheet. Bake at 375°F. for 10 to 12 minutes or until light golden brown. Cool 5 minutes. Serve warm. **8 roll-ups.**

NUTRIENTS PER 1 ROLL-UP
Calories	190	Sodium	260mg
Fat	9g	Potassium	115mg
Cholesterol	3mg		

COOK'S NOTE
Using Crescent Roll Dough

When working with crescent roll dough, keep it refrigerated until needed. Rolls or coffee cakes will be flaky and tender and will rise nicely.

Swirled Chocolate Sweet Rolls

SWIRLED CHOCOLATE SWEET ROLLS

Swirled Chocolate Sweet Rolls

These delicious sweet rolls are a must for chocolate lovers. Miniature chocolate chips make slicing the dough easier, but regular chocolate chips can be substituted.

ROLLS
- 1 package hot roll mix
- 2 tablespoons sugar
- ¼ cup unsweetened cocoa
- 1¼ cups water heated to 120 to 130°F.
- 2 tablespoons margarine or butter, softened
- 1 egg

FILLING
- 2 tablespoons margarine or butter, softened
- 2 tablespoons sugar
- ½ cup miniature semi-sweet chocolate chips

GLAZE
- Powdered sugar
- ¼ cup miniature semi-sweet chocolate chips
- 1 teaspoon shortening

Grease 13 × 9-inch pan. In large bowl, combine flour mixture with yeast from foil packet, 2 tablespoons sugar and cocoa; blend well. Stir in water, 2 tablespoons margarine and egg until dough pulls cleanly away from sides of bowl. Turn dough out onto lightly floured surface. With greased or floured hands, shape dough into a ball. Knead dough for 5 minutes until smooth. Cover with large bowl; let rest 5 minutes.

On lightly floured surface, roll dough to 15 × 12-inch rectangle. Spread with 2 tablespoons margarine. Sprinkle with 2 tablespoons sugar and ½ cup chocolate chips. Starting with 12-inch side, roll up tightly; press edges to seal. Cut into 12 slices. Place cut side down in greased pan.* Cover loosely with plastic wrap and cloth towel. Let rise 30 minutes on wire rack set over large pan to which hot water has been added.

Heat oven to 375°F. Uncover dough. Bake 15 to 20 minutes or until rolls sound hollow when lightly tapped. Immediately remove from pan. Sprinkle with powdered sugar.

In small saucepan over low heat, melt ¼ cup chocolate chips and shortening, stirring constantly until smooth. Drizzle over warm rolls. **12 rolls.**

TIP: *At this point dough can be covered with plastic wrap and refrigerated overnight. (Dough will rise in the refrigerator.) Bake as directed above.

HIGH ALTITUDE—Above 3500 Feet: No change.

NUTRIENTS PER 1 ROLL

Calories	260	Sodium	320mg
Fat	9g	Potassium	105mg
Cholesterol	25mg		

MINI-CHIP ORANGE SCONE DROPS

SCONES
   2 cups all purpose or unbleached flour
   ⅓ cup sugar
   2 teaspoons baking powder
   ½ teaspoon salt
   ¼ teaspoon baking soda
   ⅓ cup margarine or butter
   ⅓ cup orange juice
   ⅓ cup milk
   2 tablespoons grated orange peel
   ½ cup miniature semi-sweet chocolate chips

TOPPING
   3 tablespoons sugar
   ½ teaspoon cinnamon

Heat oven to 375°F. Grease cookie sheets. Lightly spoon flour into measuring cup; level off. In large bowl, combine flour, ⅓ cup sugar, baking powder, salt and baking soda; blend well. Using pastry blender or fork, cut in margarine until mixture resembles coarse crumbs. Add orange juice, milk and orange peel; stir until dry ingredients are just moistened. Stir in chocolate chips. Drop dough by heaping teaspoonfuls 2 inches apart onto greased cookie sheets.

In small bowl, combine topping ingredients; sprinkle over dough. Bake at 375°F. for 8 to 10 minutes or until light golden brown. Immediately remove from cookie sheets. Serve warm.
30 scones.

HIGH ALTITUDE – Above 3500 Feet: No change.

NUTRIENTS PER 1 SCONE

Calories	80	Sodium	90mg
Fat	3g	Potassium	30mg
Cholesterol	0mg		

CHOCOLATE RICH CRESCENT CROISSANTS

8-ounce can refrigerated crescent dinner rolls
2 tablespoons margarine or butter, softened
4-ounce bar sweet cooking chocolate
1 egg, beaten
2 tablespoons sliced or slivered almonds
   Powdered sugar
   Fudge sauce, if desired

Heat oven to 375°F. Separate dough into 8 triangles. Press each triangle to enlarge slightly; spread each with margarine. Break or cut chocolate bar into small pieces. (Chocolate may break into irregular shapes.) Place an equal amount of chocolate pieces on shortest side of each triangle. Roll up, starting at shortest side of triangle and rolling to opposite point. Place point side down on ungreased cookie sheet; curve into crescent shape. Brush each with beaten egg; sprinkle with almonds. Bake at 375°F. for 11 to 13 minutes or until golden brown. Cool completely. Sprinkle with powdered sugar. Serve fudge sauce over each croissant.
8 croissants.

NUTRIENTS PER 1 CROISSANT

Calories	220	Sodium	280mg
Fat	15g	Potassium	125mg
Cholesterol	35mg		

Mini-Chip Orange Scone Drops

Because they need no rolling, these scone drops can be made quickly. Top them warm from the oven with butter.

CHOCOLATE CHIP STREUSEL COFFEE CAKE

German Chocolate Streusel Coffee Cake

This recipe makes two scrumptious coffee cakes. Serve one warm from the oven and freeze the other to use later.

COFFEE CAKE
1 package pudding-included yellow cake mix
½ cup dairy sour cream
½ cup water
2 eggs

STREUSEL
1 cup firmly packed brown sugar
½ cup semi-sweet chocolate chips
½ cup chopped walnuts
2 tablespoons all purpose or unbleached flour
2 teaspoons cinnamon
2 tablespoons margarine or butter, melted

Heat oven to 350°F. Grease and lightly flour 13×9-inch pan. In large bowl, combine all coffee cake ingredients at low speed until moistened; beat 2 minutes at highest speed. In small bowl, combine all streusel ingredients; blend well. Spread ⅔ of batter in greased and floured pan; sprinkle with half of streusel mixture. Repeat with remaining batter and streusel mixture. Bake at 350°F. for 35 to 50 minutes or until toothpick inserted in center comes out clean. Serve warm or cool. **16 servings.**

HIGH ALTITUDE—Above 3500 Feet: Add ⅓ cup flour to dry cake mix. Increase water to ¾ cup plus 2 tablespoons. Bake as directed above.

NUTRIENTS PER 1/16 OF RECIPE

Calories	310	Sodium	260mg
Fat	13g	Potassium	170mg
Cholesterol	58mg		

GERMAN CHOCOLATE STREUSEL COFFEE CAKE

STREUSEL
½ cup all purpose or unbleached flour
⅓ cup sugar
⅓ cup margarine or butter
⅓ cup chopped pecans
⅓ cup flaked coconut
⅓ cup miniature semi-sweet chocolate chips
2 tablespoons unsweetened cocoa
½ teaspoon cinnamon

COFFEE CAKE
1 package pudding-included German chocolate or yellow cake mix
1 cup dairy sour cream
¾ cup water
3 eggs

Heat oven to 350°F. Grease and flour two 9-inch round cake pans. Lightly spoon flour into measuring cup; level off. In large bowl, combine flour and sugar; blend well. Using pastry blender or fork, cut in margarine until mixture resembles coarse crumbs. Add remaining streusel ingredients; blend well. Set aside.

In large bowl, combine all coffee cake ingredients at low speed until moistened; beat 2 minutes at highest speed. Pour half (1½ cups) of batter into each greased and floured pan. Sprinkle each evenly with half (about ½ cup) of streusel mixture. Bake at 350°F. for 35 to 40 minutes or until toothpick inserted in center comes out clean. Cool in pans 10 minutes; remove from pans. Place on serving plates, streusel side up. Serve warm or cool. **16 servings.**

HIGH ALTITUDE—Above 3500 Feet: Add ⅓ cup flour to dry cake mix. Bake as directed above.

NUTRIENTS PER 1/16 OF RECIPE

Calories	290	Sodium	260mg
Fat	14g	Potassium	105mg
Cholesterol	60mg		

Chocolate Chip Muffins

CHOCOLATE CHIP MUFFINS

MUFFINS
2 cups all purpose or unbleached flour
½ cup sugar
3 teaspoons baking powder
½ teaspoon salt
¾ cup miniature semi-sweet chocolate chips
1 egg, well beaten
¾ cup milk
⅓ cup oil

TOPPING
3 tablespoons sugar
2 tablespoons brown sugar

Heat oven to 400°F. Grease bottoms only of 12 muffin cups or line with paper baking cups. Lightly spoon flour into measuring cup; level off. In medium bowl, combine flour, ½ cup sugar, baking powder, salt and chocolate chips; blend well. Add egg, milk and oil; stir just until dry ingredients are moistened. (Batter will be lumpy.) Fill prepared muffin cups ⅔ full. In small bowl, combine topping ingredients. Sprinkle evenly over batter in each cup. Bake at 400°F. for 20 to 25 minutes or until golden brown. Run knife around sides to loosen. Remove from muffin cups immediately. Serve warm. **12 muffins.**

MICROWAVE DIRECTIONS:
Prepare muffin batter and topping as directed in recipe. Using a 6-cup microwave-safe muffin pan, line each cup with 2 paper baking cups to absorb moisture during baking. Fill paper-lined muffin cups ⅔ full. Sprinkle each evenly with about 1 teaspoonful topping. Microwave on HIGH for 1 minute. Rotate pan ½ turn. Microwave on HIGH for 1 to 1½ minutes or until toothpick inserted in center comes out clean. Remove muffins from pan; immediately discard outer paper baking cups. Repeat with remaining butter.

HIGH ALTITUDE—Above 3500 Feet: No change.

NUTRIENTS PER 1 MUFFIN

Calories	260	Sodium	180mg
Fat	11g	Potassium	95mg
Cholesterol	25mg		

CHOCOLATE CHIP MACADAMIA NUT MUFFINS

STREUSEL
¼ cup all purpose or unbleached flour
¼ cup firmly packed brown sugar
2 tablespoons margarine or butter

MUFFINS
2 cups all purpose or unbleached flour
½ cup sugar
1 teaspoon baking powder
½ teaspoon baking soda
½ teaspoon salt
¾ cup dairy sour cream
½ cup margarine or butter, melted
¼ cup milk
1 tablespoon vanilla
1 egg
½ cup chopped macadamia nuts
½ cup miniature semi-sweet chocolate chips

Heat oven to 375°F. Grease 18 muffin cups or line with paper baking cups. In small bowl, combine ¼ cup flour and brown sugar; blend well. Using pastry blender or fork, cut in 2 tablespoons margarine until mixture resembles coarse crumbs. Set aside.

Lightly spoon flour into measuring cup; level off. In large bowl, combine 2 cups flour, sugar, baking powder, baking soda and salt; blend well. Add sour cream, ½ cup margarine, milk, vanilla and egg; stir just until dry ingredients are moistened. Fold in macadamia nuts and chocolate chips.

Fill greased muffin cups ¾ full. Sprinkle each with 1½ teaspoonfuls streusel mixture. Bake at 375°F. for 18 to 20 minutes or until toothpick inserted in center comes out clean. Remove from muffin cups immediately. Serve warm. **18 muffins.**

HIGH ALTITUDE—Above 3500 Feet: Increase flour to 2 cups plus 2 tablespoons. Bake as directed above.

NUTRIENTS PER 1 MUFFIN

Calories	220	Sodium	190mg
Fat	13g	Potassium	80mg
Cholesterol	20mg		

CHOCOLATE CHIP BUBBLE BISCUITS

BISCUITS
2½ cups buttermilk complete or buttermilk pancake mix
⅓ cup sugar
½ cup miniature semi-sweet chocolate chips
⅔ cup water
⅓ cup dairy sour cream
½ teaspoon vanilla

TOPPING
¼ cup sugar
3 tablespoons finely chopped walnuts
½ teaspoon cinnamon

Heat oven to 375°F. Grease 9-inch square pan. In large bowl, combine pancake mix, ⅓ cup sugar and chocolate chips; blend well. Add water, sour cream and vanilla; blend well. On well-floured surface, form dough into 16 balls. Place balls in greased pan in 4 rows of 4 each.

In small bowl, combine all topping ingredients; blend well. Sprinkle evenly over balls of dough in pan. Bake at 375°F. for 25 to 30 minutes or until golden brown. Cool 10 minutes. Serve warm. **16 biscuits.**

HIGH ALTITUDE—Above 3500 Feet: Add ¼ cup flour to dry pancake mix. Bake as directed above.

NUTRIENTS PER 1 BISCUIT

Calories	160	Sodium	290mg
Fat	5g	Potassium	65mg
Cholesterol	2mg		

Chocolate Surprise Biscuit Ring

CHOCOLATE SURPRISE BISCUIT RING

2 (10-ounce) cans refrigerated flaky biscuits
20 milk chocolate candy kisses, unwrapped
½ cup sugar
½ teaspoon cinnamon
¼ cup margarine or butter, melted
Assorted sliced fresh fruits, if desired

Heat oven to 375°F. Generously grease 12-cup fluted tube pan. Separate dough into 20 biscuits. Press or roll out each biscuit to form 2½- to 3-inch circle. Place 1 chocolate kiss, point side up, on center of each circle. Fold dough over kiss, covering completely and forming a ball; press edges to seal.

In small bowl, combine sugar and cinnamon. Dip each ball into melted margarine; roll in sugar-cinnamon mixture. Gently place coated balls in greased pan with seams toward center. Sprinkle with any remaining sugar-cinnamon mixture; drizzle with remaining margarine. Bake at 375°F. for 25 to 35 minutes or until golden brown. Cool 1 minute; remove from pan. Just before serving, fill center of biscuit ring with fruit. Serve warm. **10 servings.**

NUTRIENTS PER 1/10 OF RECIPE

Calories	310	Sodium	660mg
Fat	15g	Potassium	75mg
Cholesterol	0mg		

Chocolate Surprise Biscuit Ring

Biscuit dough is wrapped around milk chocolate kisses to create this tempting pull-apart coffee cake. A sugar-cinnamon topping bakes into a mouth-watering glaze.

CHOCOLATE RAISIN CRESCENT TWIST

ROLLS

3-ounce package cream cheese, softened
¼ cup firmly packed brown sugar
1 egg, separated, reserving white for topping
1 teaspoon vanilla
½ cup chopped pecans
½ cup chocolate-covered raisins
8-ounce can refrigerated crescent dinner rolls

TOPPING

2 teaspoons sugar
2 teaspoons chocolate-flavored sprinkles
Reserved egg white, slightly beaten

Heat oven to 325°F. In medium bowl, combine cream cheese, brown sugar, egg yolk and vanilla; blend until smooth. Stir in pecans and chocolate-covered raisins.

Unroll dough into 2 long rectangles; firmly press perforations to seal. Press or roll out each to form 14 × 5-inch rectangle. Spread half of cream cheese mixture lengthwise down center of each rectangle to within 1 inch of edges. Starting at longest side, roll up each rectangle; press edges to seal. Place rolls 3 inches apart on ungreased cookie sheet. Press top ends of both rolls together to seal. Loosely twist, placing right roll over left, left roll over right; continue twisting down length of rolls. Press bottom ends of both rolls together to seal.

In small bowl, combine sugar and chocolate sprinkles. Brush twist with reserved beaten egg white; sprinkle with sugar mixture. Bake at 325°F. for 25 to 35 minutes or until deep golden brown. Cool 3 minutes; remove from cookie sheet. Serve warm. Store in refrigerator. **8 servings.**

NUTRIENTS PER ⅛ OF RECIPE

Calories	270	Sodium	280mg
Fat	16g	Potassium	200mg
Cholesterol	50mg		

CHOCOLATE BANANA PUFFY PANCAKES

Chocolate Banana Puffy Pancakes

The pancakes rise while baking, then fall when removed from the oven, forming a shell. This light chocolate-flavored dessert is filled with caramel-coated bananas and chocolate chips. Serve it with sweetened whipped cream for the ultimate taste sensation.

PANCAKES

½ cup all purpose or unbleached flour
2 tablespoons sugar
2 tablespoons unsweetened cocoa
2 eggs
⅔ cup milk
2 tablespoons margarine or butter

FILLING

2 tablespoons margarine or butter
⅓ cup firmly packed brown sugar
3 medium bananas, diagonally sliced
2 tablespoons miniature semi-sweet chocolate chips
1 cup whipping cream, whipped, sweetened

Heat oven to 425°F. Lightly spoon flour into measuring cup; level off. In small bowl, combine flour, sugar and cocoa; blend well. In medium bowl, beat eggs slightly. Gradually add flour mixture and milk, beating with rotary beater until smooth. Place 1 tablespoon margarine in each of two 9-inch pie pans. Heat in oven until melted; spread to cover bottom. Pour batter over melted margarine in pie pans. Bake at 425°F. for 10 to 15 minutes or until golden brown. (Edges will puff up and pancakes will form a well in center.)

In medium skillet over medium heat, melt 2 tablespoons margarine. Stir in brown sugar; bring to a boil, stirring constantly. Remove from heat; add bananas. Stir gently until bananas are well coated. Spoon half of filling into each pancake; sprinkle each with 1 tablespoon of the chocolate chips. To serve, cut each pancake into 4 wedges. Top with sweetened whipped cream. Serve immediately. **8 servings.**

NUTRIENTS PER ⅛ OF RECIPE

Calories	330	Sodium	120mg
Fat	20g	Potassium	310mg
Cholesterol	110mg		

Chocolate Waffles with Strawberries

CHOCOLATE WAFFLES WITH STRAWBERRIES

    1 cup buttermilk pancake mix
    ¼ cup unsweetened cocoa
    ⅔ cup milk
    2 tablespoons oil
    1 egg
      Whipped cream
    10-ounce package frozen
      strawberries with syrup,
      thawed*

Heat waffle iron. In medium bowl, combine pancake mix and cocoa; blend well. Add milk, oil and egg; stir until all dry particles are moistened. Bake in hot waffle iron until steaming stops. Top each waffle with whipped cream. Spoon strawberries over whipped cream. **6 waffles.**

TIP: *To make a syrup, thawed strawberries can be pureed in blender or food processor.

NUTRIENTS PER 1 WAFFLE

Calories	310	Sodium	400mg
Fat	15g	Potassium	200mg
Cholesterol	80mg		

Chocolate Waffles with Strawberries

Using a heart-shaped waffle iron will make this recipe fit a special occasion. Serve it for a company brunch or for a shortcake-like dessert.

Special Effects, Sauces & Beverages

H ere are the final flourishes for your dessert, your meal or your day. These great "endings" range from fanciful chocolate garnishes and baskets to luscious dessert sauces and sweetly satisfying chocolate beverages.

The secrets of creating special chocolate effects are now yours. And no one needs to know how easy it is to make the Chocolate Curls, Ribbons and Bows that personalize the desserts you serve. A few pieces of decorating equipment, such as a pastry bag with a variety of tips, will help ensure success. And you probably have some of the equipment already, such as cookie cutters to create Chocolate Cutouts. Once you've mastered the decorations described here, you may choose to be creative and invent some of your own.

Another way to personalize the sweets you serve is to present them in a chocolate container. A pan or mold you have on hand can be used to create a White Chocolate Lace Basket to hold candies or cookies. Tumbler bottoms partially immersed in melted chocolate candy coating create individual dessert cups. Fill each cup with fluffy white mousse and top with seasonal fresh fruits like Fruit and Cream Timbale Cups.

Chocolate is for dipping, too. In this chapter, you'll find recipes for chocolate-dipped strawberries, apricots and nuts—all lovely as garnishes or as desserts. Team them with your own dipped candies and a jar of velvet-smooth chocolate sauce as the ultimate gift to a favorite chocolate lover. Keep a jar of sauce on hand in your own kitchen, too, for topping ice cream, fruit and cake.

For a final flourish, what could be more soul-satisfying than chocolate beverages? Treat yourself to an Easy Spiced Cocoa or a Hot Chocolate Malt. When you have guests, serve After Dinner Irish Cream in chocolate Crinkle Cups that you have created. From morning to midnight, the chocolate beverages in this collection offer rich and refreshing ways to end a meal or wrap up the day.

CHOCOLATE SEASHELLS

8 ounces (8 squares) semi-sweet
or bittersweet chocolate, cut
into pieces
2 tablespoons shortening

Smoothly cover outside of eight (5 × 4-inch) seashell dishes with aluminum foil, extending foil ½ inch to inside of shell. In small saucepan over low heat, melt chocolate and shortening, stirring constantly until smooth. Remove from heat. Using flat brush or narrow spatula, brush or spread ⅛-inch layer of melted chocolate over foil on each shell. Refrigerate shells chocolate side up about 10 minutes, or until chocolate is almost set. Brush second layer of chocolate over first layer. Refrigerate until chocolate is set. Carefully loosen foil; remove from shell. Carefully peel foil away from chocolate. Store in refrigerator or freezer until ready to use. Shells can be filled with mousse, truffles or ice cream.

MICROWAVE DIRECTIONS:

In small microwave-safe bowl, combine chocolate and shortening. Microwave on MEDIUM for 3 to 4 minutes or until melted, stirring once halfway through cooking. Stir until smooth.

TIP: If chocolate shells crack, brush crack with melted chocolate to seal.

CRINKLE CUPS

Melt *semi-sweet or sweet cooking chocolate*. Using flat brush, brush melted chocolate on inside of miniature paper candy cups until about ⅛ inch thick. Wipe off any chocolate that drips over sides of cups. Refrigerate cups about 10 minutes or until chocolate is set. Brush second layer of chocolate over first layer. Refrigerate until chocolate is set. Carefully peel paper away from chocolate cups. Fill with nuts, candy or liqueur.

Various types of chocolate have different consistencies as they melt. Unsweetened chocolate becomes runny. Semi-sweet or milk chocolate holds its shape until stirred. Sweet, milk and white chocolates should be used as soon as they have melted. Unsweetened and semi-sweet chocolates should be cooled slightly before they are used in a recipe.

DOUBLE CHOCOLATE RASPBERRY SHELLS

8 Chocolate Seashells (this page)
White Chocolate Sauce (See Index)
1 pint (2 cups) raspberry sherbet
Fresh raspberries
Mint sprigs

Prepare Chocolate Seashells. To serve, place chocolate shells on individual dessert plates. Fill each shell with 3 tablespoons of White Chocolate Sauce. Place 1 scoop raspberry sherbet over sauce in each shell. Garnish each with raspberries and mint.
8 servings.

NUTRIENTS PER 1 DOUBLE CHOCOLATE RASPBERRY SHELL

Calories	450	Sodium	45mg
Fat	30g	Potassium	230mg
Cholesterol	50mg		

CHOCOLATE LEAVES

In small saucepan over low heat, melt *unsweetened, semi-sweet or sweet cooking chocolate* or *vanilla-flavored candy coating*, stirring constantly until smooth. Using flat brush, brush melted chocolate evenly on underside of washed and dried non-toxic leaves (*ivy, mint, lemon* or *rose leaves*). Wipe off any chocolate that drips to front side of leaf. Refrigerate leaves, chocolate side up, about 10 minutes or until chocolate is set. Brush second layer of chocolate over first layer. Refrigerate until chocolate is set. Carefully peel leaf away from chocolate. Place chocolate leaf on dessert, or store in refrigerator or freezer until ready to use.

Fruit and Cream Timbale Cups

FRUIT AND CREAM TIMBALE CUPS

8 ounces chocolate-flavored candy coating, cut into pieces
3 ounces (3 squares) white baking bar, cut into pieces
1 cup whipping cream
1 cup sliced fresh fruit*

Cut six 6 × 6-inch squares of foil. Using 6 tumblers (2 to 2¼ inches in diameter at base), center base of each tumbler over foil square. Wrap each tumbler base tightly with foil. In small saucepan over low heat, melt candy coating, stirring constantly until smooth. Dip each foil-wrapped tumbler in candy coating to depth of 1 inch. Allow excess to drip off. Refrigerate tumblers, candy-coated end up, about 10 minutes or until candy coating is set. Reheat candy coating as directed above. Again dip candy-coated tumblers to depth of 1 inch. Re-frigerate until candy coating is set. Carefully remove foil from tumbler. Carefully peel foil away from candy coating.

In small saucepan over low heat, melt white baking bar and whipping cream, stirring constantly until smooth. Re-frigerate whipping cream mixture about 3 hours or until very cold and thickened, stirring occasionally. Using mixer, beat chilled mixture at high speed until stiff peaks form. Spoon about ⅓ cup of whipping cream mixture into each chocolate cup. Top with about 2 tablespoons of the fruit. Serve immediately. **6 servings.**

TIP: *Use strawberries, peaches, kiwifruit, bananas, seedless grapes, blueberries, raspberries, pears or other desired fruit.

NUTRIENTS PER 1/6 OF RECIPE

Calories	450	Sodium	55mg
Fat	34g	Potassium	210mg
Cholesterol	60mg		

Fruit and Cream Timbale Cups

Tumbler bottoms are dipped into melted chocolate candy coating to create appealing individual dessert cups. Each cup is filled with a fluffy white chocolate mousse and topped with seasonal fresh fruits.

CHOCOLATE CURLS

4 ounces (4 squares) semi-sweet chocolate or white baking bar*

In small saucepan over low heat, melt chocolate, stirring constantly until smooth. With spatula, spread melted chocolate in thin layer on inverted cookie sheets. Refrigerate just until firm but not brittle, about 10 minutes. Using metal spatula or pancake turner, scrape chocolate from pan, forming curls. (Chocolate curls will be as wide as spatula.) Transfer curls to dessert with toothpick, or store in refrigerator or freezer until ready to use.

TIP: *A chocolate bar can be used to make chocolate curls. Let chocolate bar (any type) stand in warm place (80 to 85°F.) until slightly softened, about 10 minutes. Using vegetable peeler, shave chocolate in long strands along smooth side of chocolate. For large curls, pull peeler along narrow side of chocolate. Continue as directed in recipe.

Marbled Chocolate Curls: In small saucepan over low heat, melt chocolate, stirring constantly until smooth. In another small saucepan, melt *4 ounces vanilla-flavored candy coating*, stirring constantly until smooth. With spatula, spread melted chocolate and candy coating in thin marbled layer on inverted cookie sheet. Continue as directed in recipe.

Pattern for Chocolate Filigree Hearts

CHOCOLATE PIPING

2 ounces (2 squares) semi-sweet or sweet cooking chocolate
2 teaspoons margarine

In small saucepan over low heat, melt chocolate and margarine, stirring constantly until smooth. Cool 15 minutes. Pour chocolate into small squeeze bottle or pastry bag fitted with writing tip. Pipe a design directly on dessert.

White Chocolate Piping: Substitute *vanilla-flavored candy coating* for semi-sweet chocolate. *Omit margarine.* Continue as directed in recipe.

Chocolate Filigree: Melt chocolate as directed in recipe, substituting *1½ teaspoons shortening* for margarine. Pour chocolate into small squeeze bottle or pastry bag fitted with small writing tip. Pipe designs onto waxed paper-lined cookie sheets. Refrigerate just until firm but not brittle, about 10 minutes. Transfer filigrees with metal spatula or pancake turner from waxed paper-lined cookie sheet to dessert, or store in refrigerator or freezer until ready to use.

Chocolate Filigree Hearts: Draw 1 heart pattern on white paper. Cut twelve 3 × 3-inch squares of waxed paper. Set aside. Melt chocolate as directed in recipe, substituting *2 teaspoons shortening* for margarine. Pour chocolate mixture into small squeeze bottle or pastry bag fitted with small writing tip. Place heart pattern on cookie sheet. Lay 1 square waxed paper over pattern. Pipe chocolate onto waxed paper, following heart pattern. (Chocolate lines should be about ¼ inch wide.) Carefully slip out heart pattern to reuse. Repeat to make 12 filigree hearts. Refrigerate 30 minutes or until ready to use. Carefully remove waxed paper; place each heart on dessert.
12 filigree hearts.

WHITE CHOCOLATE ROSES

In small saucepan over low heat, melt 4 ounces *vanilla-flavored candy coating*, stirring constantly until smooth. Stir in 2 tablespoons *corn syrup*; cool. Wrap mixture in plastic wrap; let stand at room temperature at least 4 hours or overnight. Knead mixture until smooth. Shape mixture into about forty to fifty ¼ to ½-inch balls. Place balls 1 inch apart on 2 waxed paper-lined cookie sheets. Press balls with fingers to flatten into circles. Cover with waxed paper. Refrigerate 10 to 15 minutes for easier handling.

To form rose, roll 1 of the small circles tightly to form center. Build on center to form outer petals by wrapping remaining circles around center, overlapping slightly. Press together at base. Curl out tops of outer edges like rose petals. Roses can be made in various sizes. Flatten bottom slightly; refrigerate until firm. Place on dessert, or store in refrigerator or freezer until ready to use. **15 to 20 roses.**

WHITE CHOCOLATE SWANS

Draw body and wings of swan pattern onto waxed paper. Repeat pattern 2 or 3 times. Place waxed paper patterns on cookie sheet. In small saucepan over low heat, melt 6 ounces *vanilla-flavored candy coating*, stirring constantly until smooth. Pour candy coating into pastry bag fitted with #5 or #6 writing tip. Pipe candy coating on waxed paper following swan patterns and filling in wing area. Refrigerate 15 minutes or until candy coating is set. Place body of 1 swan in empty egg carton. To attach wings to body, pipe a small amount of candy coating on inside of each of 2 wings. Place in egg carton next to body of swan; press gently at bottom to secure. Allow wings to fall away slightly from body, using egg carton as support. Repeat with other swan bodies and wings. Place on dessert, or store in refrigerator or freezer until ready to use. **3 to 4 swans.**

COOK'S NOTE
White Chocolate

White chocolate is a misnomer. It is not considered chocolate in the U.S. by the Food and Drug Administration because it does not contain chocolate liqueur from the cocoa bean.

Pattern for White Chocolate Swans

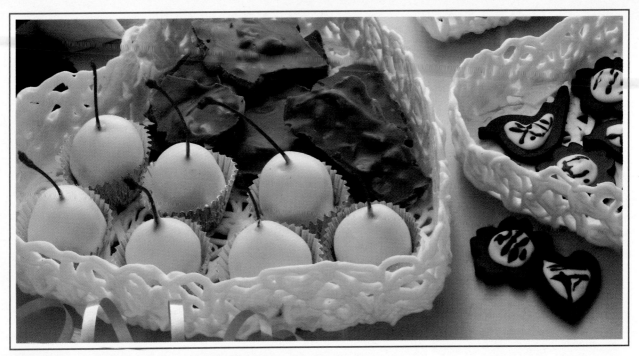

Pictured left to right: *White Chocolate Lace Baskets; White Chocolate-Covered Cherries, page 132; Milk Chocolate Peanut Butter Bark, page 109; White and Dark Chocolate Cutouts*

WHITE CHOCOLATE LACE BASKET

6 ounces vanilla-flavored candy coating

Press piece of foil firmly over outside of 8-inch heart-shaped cake pan. Place foil-covered pan in freezer.

In small saucepan over low heat, melt candy coating, stirring constantly until smooth. Cool slightly. Pour melted coating into small squeeze bottle or pastry bag fitted with small writing tip. Drizzle coating randomly over bottom and sides of chilled foil-covered pan. Apply heavier coating on edges and corners. Freeze coated pan 30 minutes.

Unmold basket by *carefully* lifting foil from pan. *Carefully* peel foil away from basket. Place on serving tray. Refrigerate until ready to use. Fill with candies or cookies. **1 basket.**

TIP: If basket breaks, mend with melted candy coating.

White Chocolate Lace Basket

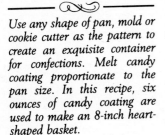

Use any shape of pan, mold or cookie cutter as the pattern to create an exquisite container for confections. Melt candy coating proportionate to the pan size. In this recipe, six ounces of candy coating are used to make an 8-inch heart-shaped basket.

CHOCOLATE CUTOUTS

6 ounces (6 squares) semi-sweet or sweet cooking chocolate

In small saucepan over low heat, melt chocolate, stirring constantly until smooth. Pour onto waxed paper-lined cookie sheet. Spread evenly to ⅛ to ¼-inch thickness. Refrigerate just until firm but not brittle, about 10 minutes. To make cutouts, press small cookie or canape cutters firmly into chocolate. Lift cutouts gently from waxed paper with metal spatula or pancake turner. Place on dessert, or store in refrigerator or freezer until ready to use.

Chocolate Diamonds: Prepare chocolate as directed in recipe. Using sharp knife, cut chocolate into diamond shapes. Continue as directed in recipe.

Chocolate Wedges: Melt chocolate as directed in recipe. Pour onto waxed paper-lined cookie sheet. With spatula, spread evenly to form a circle ⅛ to ¼ inch thick. Refrigerate until firm but not brittle, about 10 minutes. Using sharp knife, cut circle into 8 to 12 wedges. Continue as directed in recipe.

WHITE AND DARK CHOCOLATE CUTOUTS

3 ounces (3 squares) white baking bar, chopped
6 ounces (6 squares) semi-sweet chocolate, chopped

Line cookie sheet with waxed paper. In small saucepan over low heat, melt white baking bar, stirring constantly until smooth. Set aside.

In another small saucepan over low heat, melt semi-sweet chocolate, stirring constantly until smooth.

Reserve 2 tablespoons of the melted semi-sweet chocolate for garnish. Pour remaining melted semi-sweet chocolate onto waxed paper-lined cookie sheet. Using spatula, spread to ⅛-inch thickness. Refrigerate until firm but not brittle, about 10 minutes.

To make cutouts, press small cookie or canape cutters firmly into chocolate. Spoon a small amount of melted white baking bar in center of each cutout; spread almost to edge.

Drizzle cutouts with reserved 2 tablespoons melted semi-sweet chocolate. Refrigerate until firm. With spatula, gently lift cutouts from waxed paper. Store candy between layers of waxed paper in covered container in refrigerator. **8 ounces candy** (about 60 pieces).

CANDY MINT TREES

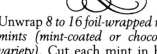

Unwrap *8 to 16 foil-wrapped rectangular mints (mint-coated or chocolate-coated variety)*. Cut each mint in half diagonally. Position triangular mint pieces side by side to create tree shape. Use 2, 3 or 4 triangular pieces to create flat or 3-dimensional trees. Small squares can be cut from mints to form tree trunks. Use to garnish cakes or other desserts.

CHOCOLATE RIBBONS AND BOWS

6-ounce package (1 cup) semi-sweet chocolate chips
¼ cup corn syrup
Unsweetened cocoa

In small saucepan over low heat, melt chocolate chips with corn syrup, stirring constantly until smooth. Refrigerate 45 to 60 minutes or until mixture is firm enough to knead. Knead well, 1 to 2 minutes. Place mixture on surface lightly sprinkled with cocoa. Roll out to 18 × 6-inch rectangle, about ⅛ inch thick. With fluted pastry roller or knife, cut into ¾-inch-wide strips. Use some strips for ribbons; fold some strips to form bows. Transfer ribbons and bows with spatula to dessert.

TIP: For ease of handling, roll out chocolate mixture between 2 sheets of parchment paper dusted lightly with cocoa.

GRATED CHOCOLATE

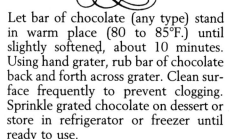

Let bar of chocolate (any type) stand in warm place (80 to 85°F.) until slightly softened, about 10 minutes. Using hand grater, rub bar of chocolate back and forth across grater. Clean surface frequently to prevent clogging. Sprinkle grated chocolate on dessert or store in refrigerator or freezer until ready to use.

CHOCOLATE SHAVINGS

Let bar of chocolate (any type) stand in warm place (80 to 85°F.) until slightly softened, about 10 minutes. Pull a vegetable peeler against smooth side of chocolate using short, quick strokes. Transfer shavings to dessert with toothpick or store in refrigerator or freezer until ready to use.

APRICOT DOUBLE DIPS

½ cup semi-sweet chocolate chips
2 tablespoons margarine or butter
6-oz. pkg. dried apricots
½ cup vanilla milk chips

Line cookie sheets with waxed paper. In small saucepan over low heat, melt chocolate chips and margarine; stir until smooth. Remove from heat. Set saucepan in pan of warm water to maintain dipping consistency. Dip 1 end of each apricot in chocolate mixture. Place on prepared cookie sheets. Refrigerate to set chocolate coating.

Meanwhile, in small saucepan over low heat, melt vanilla milk chips; stir until smooth. Set saucepan in pan of warm water to maintain dipping consistency. Dip coated end of each apricot in melted vanilla chips to within ¼ inch of top edge of chocolate coating. Place on prepared cookie sheets. Refrigerate to set vanilla coating. Place in paper candy cups. Cover; store in cool place. **40 to 45 pieces**

MICROWAVE DIRECTIONS:

In 4-cup microwave-safe measuring cup, combine chocolate chips and margarine. Microwave on HIGH for 45 to 60 seconds or until melted; stir until smooth. Continue as directed above. In 4-cup microwave-safe measuring cup, place vanilla milk chips. Microwave on HIGH for 45 to 60 seconds or until melted; stir until smooth. Continue as directed above.

NUTRIENTS PER 1 PIECE

Calories	35	Sodium	10 mg
Fat	2g	Potassium	65mg
Cholesterol	0mg		

WHITE CHOCOLATE-COVERED CHERRIES

2 (10-ounce) jars maraschino cherries with stems

FONDANT
¼ cup butter, softened
1 tablespoon cherry-flavored liqueur
1 tablespoon light corn syrup
2 cups powdered sugar

COATING
24 ounces vanilla-flavored candy coating, chopped

Drain cherries; let dry on paper towels overnight. Line cookie sheet with waxed paper. In small bowl, combine butter, liqueur and corn syrup; blend well. Stir in powdered sugar; knead until smooth. Shape heaping ½ teaspoonful fondant around each cherry, covering completely. Place on waxed paper-lined cookie sheet; refrigerate.

In small saucepan over low heat, melt candy coating, stirring constantly until smooth. Remove from heat. Set saucepan in hot water to maintain dipping consistency. Hold cherries by stems; dip quickly into melted coating, covering completely. Place on waxed paper-lined cookie sheet. Refrigerate for 30 minutes to set. Dip each coated cherry a second time in melted coating. Reheat coating over low heat if necessary. Refrigerate double-dipped cherries to set. Store in covered container at room temperature for 2 weeks to allow fondant to liquefy. **40 cherries.**

NUTRIENTS PER 1 CHERRY

Calories	130	Sodium	15mg
Fat	7g	Potassium	55mg
Cholesterol	2mg		

White Chocolate-Covered Cherries

It takes about two weeks for the fondant in this recipe to ripen or liquefy, so you will need to make the candies early. For an extra-special gift, make a small White Chocolate Lace Basket (see Index) and fill it with these tempting confections.

Chocolate-Dipped Strawberries

CHOCOLATE-DIPPED STRAWBERRIES

2 pints strawberries, unhulled
½ cup semi-sweet chocolate chips
1 tablespoon corn syrup
1 tablespoon rum, if desired
5 teaspoons margarine or butter

Wash strawberries; gently pat dry. Place on paper towels until room temperature. In small saucepan over low heat, melt chocolate chips with corn syrup, rum and margarine, stirring constantly until smooth. Remove from heat. Set saucepan in hot water to maintain dipping consistency. Dip each strawberry in chocolate mixture until ⅔ of strawberry is coated. Allow excess to drip off. Place hull side down on waxed paper-lined cookie sheets. Refrigerate until chocolate is set, about 15 minutes. Best when served within 3 to 4 hours. **36 to 48 strawberries.**

NUTRIENTS PER 1 STRAWBERRY

Calories	18	Sodium	5mg
Fat	1g	Potassium	30mg
Cholesterol	0mg		

Chocolate-Dipped Strawberries

Serve these chocolate-dipped treats on your cookie and candy tray, or use them as a garnish for desserts.

CHOCOLATE-DIPPED NUTS

2 ounces (2 squares) semi-sweet chocolate
2 cups whole almonds, walnut halves or pecan halves

Line cookie sheets with waxed paper. In small saucepan over low heat, melt chocolate, stirring constantly until smooth. Remove from heat. Set saucepan in hot water to maintain dipping consistency. Dip half of each nut in melted chocolate. Allow excess to drip off. Place on waxed paper-lined cookie sheets. Refrigerate until chocolate is set. If desired, place in paper candy cups. Store in refrigerator. **2 cups.**

Chocolate-Dipped Cherries or Grapes: Melt chocolate as directed in recipe adding *1 tablespoon shortening.* Substitute *cherries with stems* or *small clusters of seedless grapes* for nuts. Continue as directed in recipe.

Chocolate-Dipped Mandarin Oranges: Melt chocolate as directed in recipe adding *1 teaspoon shortening.* Toast *½ cup coconut* by spreading on cookie sheet. Bake at 350°F. for about 5 minutes or until light golden brown, stirring occasionally. Or, spread in a thin layer in microwave-safe pie pan. Microwave on LOW for 4½ to 8 minutes or until light golden brown, tossing with fork after each minute. (Moist flaked coconut takes longer than drier shredded coconut.) Substitute *11-ounce can mandarin orange segments,* drained, for nuts. Dip 1 end of each orange segment in chocolate, then in toasted coconut. Continue as directed in recipe.

NUTRIENTS PER 2 TABLESPOONS CHOCOLATE-DIPPED NUTS

Calories	140	Sodium	0mg
Fat	11g	Potassium	140mg
Cholesterol	0mg		

ROYAL FONDUE

FONDUE

¾ cup sugar
¾ cup whipping cream
8 ounces milk chocolate, broken into pieces
2 tablespoons margarine or butter
1 tablespoon light corn syrup

DIPPERS

Apple wedges
Banana chunks
Large marshmallows
Maraschino cherries
Orange sections
Pineapple chunks
Pound cake cubes
Wafer cookies

In medium saucepan, combine all fondue ingredients. Bring to a boil over medium heat, stirring constantly. Reduce heat; simmer 5 minutes, stirring occasionally. Pour mixture into fondue pot; keep warm over low heat. Spear dippers with fondue forks; dip into fondue. **2½ cups.**

MICROWAVE DIRECTIONS:
In 1-quart microwave-safe bowl, combine sugar and whipping cream; blend well. Microwave on HIGH for 2 minutes. Add chocolate, margarine and corn syrup; stir. Microwave on HIGH for 2½ to 4 minutes or until mixture comes to a boil, stirring well every minute.

NUTRIENTS PER 1 TABLESPOON FONDUE

Calories	60	Sodium	15mg
Fat	3g	Potassium	30mg
Cholesterol	4mg		

Quick Chocolate Peanut Butter Cookie Pops

QUICK CHOCOLATE PEANUT BUTTER COOKIE POPS

20 vanilla wafers
¼ cup peanut butter
10 wooden sticks
5 ounces chocolate-flavored candy
  coating

To assemble each cookie pop, spread about 1 teaspoon of the peanut butter over flat side of 1 vanilla wafer. Press end of 1 wooden stick into peanut butter. Top with 1 plain vanilla wafer, placing flat sides together. Repeat for remaining cookie pops.

In small saucepan over low heat, melt candy coating, stirring constantly until smooth. Set saucepan in hot water to maintain dipping consistency. Dip cookie pops in candy coating.* Allow excess to drip off. Place on waxed paper until set. **10 cookie pops.**

MICROWAVE DIRECTIONS:
Assemble cookie pops as directed above. Place candy coating in 2-cup microwave-safe measuring cup. Microwave on MEDIUM for 3 minutes or until melted, stirring once halfway through cooking. Stir until smooth. Continue as directed above.

TIP: *For easier dipping, pour melted candy coating into glass measuring cup or other tall, narrow container.

Dip-a-Cookie Treats: Omit peanut butter and wooden sticks. Melt candy coating as directed in recipe. Choose any of the following cookies and dip each halfway into coating: cream-filled vanilla, chocolate or peanut butter sandwich cookies, vanilla wafers, shortbread cookies, sugar wafers, coconut bar cookies or fig bars. Allow excess candy coating to drip off. Place on waxed paper until set.

NUTRIENTS PER 1 COOKIE POP

Calories	160	Sodium	60mg
Fat	10g	Potassium	80mg
Cholesterol	2mg		

Quick Chocolate Peanut Butter Cookie Pops

Fun-loving folks of all ages will enjoy making and eating these unbelievably easy, great-tasting cookie pops. Creamy peanut butter is spread between two crisp vanilla wafers, which are then dipped in melted chocolate.

Satin Fudge Sauce

SATIN FUDGE SAUCE

1½ cups powdered sugar
⅓ cup butter or margarine
4 ounces (4 squares) semi-sweet chocolate, chopped
5-ounce can (about ½ cup) evaporated milk
1 teaspoon vanilla

In medium heavy saucepan, combine all ingredients except vanilla. Bring to a boil over medium heat, stirring constantly. Reduce heat; simmer 5 minutes, stirring constantly. Remove from heat; stir in vanilla. Serve warm over ice cream or dessert. Store in refrigerator. 1⅔ cups.

MICROWAVE DIRECTIONS:
In medium microwave-safe bowl, combine all ingredients except vanilla. Microwave on HIGH for 4 to 5 minutes or until mixture comes to a boil, stirring every 2 minutes. Microwave on LOW for 2 to 3 minutes, stirring once during cooking. Continue as directed above.

NUTRIENTS PER 1 TABLESPOON

Calories	80	Sodium	30mg
Fat	4g	Potassium	35mg
Cholesterol	7mg		

WHITE CHOCOLATE SAUCE

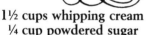

1½ cups whipping cream
¼ cup powdered sugar
4 ounces (4 squares) white baking bar, cut into pieces
2 tablespoons rum

In medium saucepan, combine whipping cream and powdered sugar; blend well. Bring to a boil over medium heat, stirring constantly. Reduce heat; simmer 3 to 4 minutes, stirring occasionally. Remove from heat. Add white baking bar and rum; stir until chocolate is melted and sauce is smooth. Serve warm or cool. Store in refrigerator. 2 cups.

MICROWAVE DIRECTIONS:
In 4-cup microwave-safe measuring cup, combine powdered sugar and whipping cream; blend well. Microwave on HIGH for 3½ to 4 minutes or until mixture comes to a boil, stirring once during cooking. Add white baking bar and rum; stir until chocolate is melted and sauce is smooth.

NUTRIENTS PER 1 TABLESPOON

Calories	60	Sodium	5mg
Fat	5g	Potassium	20mg
Cholesterol	16mg		

CHOCO-MINT SAUCE

3 tablespoons margarine or butter
⅓ cup unsweetened cocoa
1 cup powdered sugar
½ cup evaporated skim milk
½ teaspoon mint extract

In small saucepan over medium heat, melt margarine. Remove from heat. Stir in cocoa; blend well. Gradually stir in powdered sugar and milk. Cook over medium heat until powdered sugar is dissolved and sauce thickens and begins to bubble, stirring constantly. Cool slightly. Stir in mint extract. Serve warm over ice cream or dessert. Store in refrigerator. 1 cup.

MICROWAVE DIRECTIONS:
Place margarine in 4-cup microwave-safe measuring cup. Microwave on HIGH for 30 to 45 seconds or until melted. Stir in cocoa; blend well. Gradually stir in powdered sugar and milk. Microwave on HIGH for 2 to 3 minutes or until powdered sugar is dissolved and sauce thickens and begins to bubble, stirring with wire whisk halfway through cooking. Cool slightly. Stir in mint extract. Serve warm over ice cream or dessert.

NUTRIENTS PER 1 TABLESPOON

Calories	60	Sodium	45mg
Fat	3g	Potassium	40mg
Cholesterol	0mg		

Satin Fudge Sauce

This recipe makes almost two cups of sauce and any left over stores well refrigerated in a covered container. When microwave directions are available for sauces, you can be assured of a smooth sauce without constant stirring.

CHOCOLATE PRALINE ICE CREAM TOPPING

2/3 cup firmly packed brown sugar
1 cup whipping cream
2/3 cup butter or margarine
6-ounce package (1 cup) semi-sweet chocolate chips
1 cup pecan halves

In medium saucepan, combine brown sugar, whipping cream and butter. Bring to a boil over medium heat, stirring constantly. Reduce heat; simmer 2 minutes, stirring occasionally. Add chocolate chips; stir until melted and smooth. Stir in pecans. Serve warm over ice cream or dessert. Store in refrigerator. **3 cups.**

MICROWAVE DIRECTIONS:

In 4-cup microwave-safe measuring cup, combine brown sugar, whipping cream and butter. Microwave on HIGH for 4 to 4½ minutes or until mixture comes to a full boil, stirring once halfway through cooking. Add chocolate chips; stir until melted and smooth. Stir in pecans. Continue as directed above.

NUTRIENTS PER 2 TABLESPOONS
Calories	170	Sodium	60mg
Fat	14g	Potassium	70mg
Cholesterol	25mg		

Chocolate Praline Ice Cream Topping

Include a jar of this superb topping with a gift of an ice cream maker, or tuck a jar into a gift basket for chocolate lovers.

CHOCOLATE HONEY BUTTER

½ cup butter or margarine, softened
2 tablespoons honey
2 tablespoons chocolate-flavored syrup

In small bowl, combine all ingredients. Beat at high speed until light and fluffy. **1 cup.**

NUTRIENTS PER 1 TABLESPOON
Calories	70	Sodium	60mg
Fat	6g	Potassium	10mg
Cholesterol	15mg		

CHOCOLATE CARAMEL SAUCE

½ cup whipping cream
1 tablespoon margarine or butter
6-ounce package (1 cup) semi-sweet chocolate chips
12 caramels, unwrapped
Sliced apples or favorite fresh fruit

In small saucepan, combine whipping cream, margarine, chocolate chips and caramels. Cook over low heat, stirring occasionally until smooth. Serve warm over fruit. Store in refrigerator. **1⅓ cups.**

MICROWAVE DIRECTIONS:

In small microwave-safe bowl, combine whipping cream and caramels. Microwave on MEDIUM for 4½ to 5 minutes, stirring once during cooking. Stir until mixture is smooth. Add margarine and chocolate chips; stir until smooth.

NUTRIENTS PER 1 TABLESPOON
Calories	90	Sodium	20mg
Fat	6g	Potassium	40mg
Cholesterol	8mg		

ULTIMATE CHOCOLATE MALT

½ cup milk or chocolate milk
4 tablespoons chocolate-flavored syrup
4 tablespoons chocolate malted milk powder
1 quart (4 cups) chocolate ice cream, softened

In blender container, combine milk, chocolate syrup and malted milk powder; blend 10 seconds. Add ice cream; blend until smooth. Pour into glasses; serve immediately. **4 (1-cup) servings.**

NUTRIENTS PER 1/4 OF RECIPE
Calories	370	Sodium	160mg
Fat	16g	Potassium	400mg
Cholesterol	60mg		

CHERRY-CHOCOLATE DRINK

¾ cup milk
2 tablespoons chocolate-flavored syrup
1 tablespoon maraschino cherry juice
2 tablespoons whipped cream
Long-stemmed maraschino cherry

MICROWAVE DIRECTIONS:
In microwave-safe mug, combine milk, chocolate-flavored syrup and maraschino cherry juice; blend well. Microwave on HIGH for 2 to 2½ minutes or until hot. Top with whipped cream and long-stemmed maraschino cherry.
1 serving.

NUTRIENTS PER 1 SERVING

Calories	270	Sodium	115mg
Fat	10g	Potassium	420mg
Cholesterol	35mg		

FLAVORED MOCHA MIXES

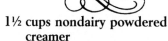

1½ cups nondairy powdered creamer
1 cup sugar
½ cup instant coffee granules or crystals
½ cup unsweetened cocoa
Dash salt
¼ teaspoon vanilla
¼ teaspoon almond extract
Boiling water
Whipped cream, if desired

In large bowl, combine nondairy powdered creamer, sugar, instant coffee, cocoa and salt; blend well. Place 1½ cups of mixture in small bowl. Add vanilla; blend well. Add almond extract to remaining mixture in large bowl; blend well. Store each in tightly covered container.

To serve, combine 3 tablespoons of desired mix with 1 cup boiling water; stir to blend. Top with whipped cream.
1½ cups of each flavor of mix.

NUTRIENTS PER 1/8 OF RECIPE

Calories	130	Sodium	45mg
Fat	6g	Potassium	135mg
Cholesterol	10mg		

AFTER DINNER IRISH CREAM

2 cups whipping cream
1¾ cups brandy
14-ounce can sweetened condensed milk (not evaporated)
2 tablespoons chocolate-flavored syrup
1½ teaspoons vanilla

In blender container, combine all ingredients; blend at low speed until foamy. Serve immediately or cover and refrigerate up to 1 week. Blend or shake well before serving.
18 (⅓-cup) servings.

NUTRIENTS PER 1/18 OF RECIPE

Calories	260	Sodium	60mg
Fat	13g	Potassium	150mg
Cholesterol	90mg		

EASY SPICED COCOA

½ cup unsweetened cocoa
½ teaspoon cinnamon
¼ teaspoon nutmeg
14-ounce can sweetened condensed milk (not evaporated)
1 teaspoon vanilla
4½ cups water heated to 115 to 120°F.
Whipped cream

In large saucepan, combine cocoa, cinnamon and nutmeg. Stir in milk and vanilla. Add water; blend well. Cook over low heat until thoroughly heated, stirring occasionally. *Do not boil.* Blend well; pour into cups or mugs. Top with whipped cream. **12 (½-cup) servings.**

NUTRIENTS PER 1/12 OF RECIPE

Calories	180	Sodium	85mg
Fat	7g	Potassium	200mg
Cholesterol	25mg		

After Dinner Irish Cream

Serve this in Crinkle Cups (see Index) or pour it into a decorative bottle to give as a gift to special friends.

COOK'S NOTE
Heating Beverages in the Microwave

When microwaving beverages, use only microwave-safe cups or mugs. Avoid fine china, questionable plastics and containers with metal trim or with paints and glazes containing metallic substances.

Keep beverages from boiling over by using a cup, mug or other container that is large enough to allow for bubbling during heating.

Watch the time carefully. Begin with the least amount of time stated and add seconds in intervals if necessary.

Pictured clockwise from left: Cherry-Chocolate Drink, page 139; Hot Chocolate Malt; Marshmallowy Chocolate Milk

HOT CHOCOLATE MALT

1 cup chocolate milk
2 teaspoons chocolate malted milk
   powder
Vanilla ice cream

MICROWAVE DIRECTIONS:
In microwave-safe mug, combine chocolate milk and chocolate malted milk powder; blend well. Microwave on HIGH for 2 to 2½ minutes or until hot. Stir until smooth. Add scoop of vanilla ice cream. **1 serving.**

NUTRIENTS PER 1 SERVING

Calories	330	Sodium	220mg
Fat	12g	Potassium	570mg
Cholesterol	45mg		

MARSHMALLOWY CHOCOLATE MILK

1 cup chocolate milk
4 tablespoons marshmallow creme
   Miniature chocolate chips

MICROWAVE DIRECTIONS:
In large microwave-safe mug, combine chocolate milk and 2 tablespoons of the marshmallow creme; blend well. Microwave on HIGH for 2 to 2½ minutes or until hot. Stir to dissolve marshmallow creme. Top with remaining 2 tablespoons of marshmallow creme; sprinkle with chocolate chips.
1 serving.

NUTRIENTS PER 1 SERVING

Calories	300	Sodium	160mg
Fat	7g	Potassium	440mg
Cholesterol	15mg		

Appendix

Nutrition Information

Pillsbury recipe analysis is provided per serving or per unit of food and is based on the most current nutritional values available from the United States Department of Agriculture (USDA). Each recipe is calculated for number of calories, grams of fat, and milligrams of cholesterol, sodium and potassium. If you are following a medically prescribed diet, consult your physician or registered dietitian about using this information.

CALCULATING NUTRITION INFORMATION: Recipe analysis is based on:

- A single serving based on the largest number of servings, or on a specific amount (1 tablespoon) or unit (1 cookie).

- The first ingredient or amount when more than one is listed.

- "If desired" or garnishing ingredients when they are included in the ingredient listing.

USING NUTRITION INFORMATION: The amount of nutrients a person needs is determined by one's age, size and activity level. Pillsbury has used the U.S. recommended daily allowance for women ages twenty-three to fifty as its guidelines for recipe analysis. Men, teenagers and pregnant or nursing women generally need more of some nutrients.

Guidelines used:
Calories: 1800 to 2400
Fat: 67 grams or less
Cholesterol: 300 milligrams or less
Sodium: 1100 to 3300 milligrams

A nutritionally balanced diet recommends limiting fat to 30 percent or less of total daily calories. One gram of fat is 9 calories. You can determine the fat content of recipes or products with the following formula:

$$\frac{\text{GRAMS OF FAT PER SERVING} \times 9}{\text{TOTAL CALORIES PER SERVING}} = \frac{\text{PERCENT}}{\text{OF CALORIES}}_{\text{FROM FAT}}$$

Pillsbury Products Used in the Recipes in this Book

DRY GROCERY PRODUCTS:

Flour
Pillsbury's BEST® All Purpose Flour
Pillsbury's BEST® Unbleached All Purpose Flour

Frosting
Pillsbury Chocolate Chip Frosting Supreme™
Pillsbury Chocolate Fudge Frosting Supreme™
Pillsbury Coconut Pecan Frosting Supreme™
Pillsbury Milk Chocolate Frosting Supreme™

Mixes
Brownies:
Pillsbury Fudge Brownie Mix
Cake:
Pillsbury Plus® Dark Chocolate Cake Mix
Pillsbury Plus® Devil's Food Cake Mix
Pillsbury Plus® Fudge Marble Cake Mix
Pillsbury Plus® German Chocolate Cake Mix
Pillsbury Plus® White Cake Mix
Pillsbury Plus® Yellow Cake Mix
Specialty:
Hungry Jack® Buttermilk Complete Pancake Mix
Hungry Jack® Buttermilk Pancake and Waffle Mix
Pillsbury Hot Roll Mix

REFRIGERATED PRODUCTS:

Hungry Jack® Refrigerated Flaky Biscuits
Pillsbury All Ready Pie Crusts
Pillsbury Refrigerated Quick Crescent Dinner Rolls

Index